Elementary Education: Content Knowledge Study Guide

▶ ▶ ▶ ▶ ▶ ▶ ▶ ▶ ▶ ▶ ▶ ▶

A PUBLICATION OF EDUCATIONAL TESTING SERVICE

Table of Contents

Study Guide for the *Elementary Education: Content Knowledge* Test

▶   ▶   ▶   ▶   ▶   ▶   ▶   ▶   ▶   ▶   ▶   ▶

TABLE OF CONTENTS

Please take a moment to complete a review of the Elementary Education: Content Knowledge Study Guide. There is a preaddressed feedback form included on the final page of this guide. Thank you in advance for your comments.

Chapter 1

Introduction to *Elementary Education:*
Content Knowledge and Suggestions for
Using this Study Guide

▶ ▶ ▶ ▶ ▶ ▶ ▶ ▶ ▶ ▶ ▶ ▶

Introduction to the *Elementary Education: Content Knowledge* Test

The *Elementary Education: Content Knowledge* test is designed for prospective teachers of children in primary through upper elementary school grades. The 120 multiple-choice questions focus on four major subject areas:

- Language Arts and Reading

- Mathematics

- Social Studies

- Science

The test questions are arranged in the test book by subject area. Each of the four content areas constitutes 25 percent of the test. You will have two hours to complete the test.

The test is not intended to be a test of your teaching skills. It is intended to demonstrate that you possess fundamental knowledge in the subject areas you will be required to teach.

Suggestions for Using the "Study Topics" Chapters

This test is different from a final exam or other tests you may have taken in that it is comprehensive — that is, it covers four different content areas and it covers material you may have learned in several courses during more than one year. It requires you to synthesize information you have learned from numerous sources and to understand the subjects as a whole.

As a teacher, you will need a thorough understanding of the fundamental concepts in these four subject areas and the ways in which the various concepts fit together. You also need to understand typical misconceptions, because you will need to apply your knowledge to situations in the classroom.

This test is very different from the SAT® or other assessments of your reading, writing, and mathematical skills. You may have heard it said that you can't study for the SAT — that is, you should have learned these skills throughout your school years, and you can't learn reading or reasoning skills shortly before you take the exam. The *Elementary Education: Content Knowledge* test assesses a domain you can review for and can prepare to be tested on. Moreover, studying for your licensing exam is a great opportunity to reflect on your field and develop a deeper understanding of it before you begin to teach the subject matter to others.

We recommend the following approach for using the "Study Topics" chapters to prepare for the test.

Become familiar with the test content. Learn what will be tested in the four sections of the test, covered in chapters 3-6.

Assess how well you know the content in each area. It is quite likely that you will need to study in most or all of the four content areas. After you learn what the test contains, you should assess your knowledge in each area. How well do you know the material? In which areas do you need to learn more before you take the test?

Develop a study plan. Assess what you need to study and create a realistic plan for studying. You can develop your study plan in any way that works best for you. A "Study Plan" form is included in Appendix A at the end of the book as a possible way to structure your planning. Remember that this is a licensure test and covers a great deal of material. Plan to review carefully. You will need to allow time to find the books and other materials, time to read the material and take notes, and time to go over your notes.

Identify study materials. Most of the material covered by the test is contained in standard introductory textbooks in each of the four fields. If you do not own an introductory text in each area, you may want to borrow one or more from friends or from a library. You may also want to obtain a copy of your state's standards for the subject areas for elementary-grade students. (One way to find these standards quickly is to go to the Web site for your state's Department of Education.) The textbooks used in elementary classrooms may also prove useful to you, since they also present the material you need to know. Use standard school and college introductory textbooks and other reliable, professionally prepared materials. Don't rely heavily on information provided by friends or from searching the World Wide Web. Neither of these sources is as uniformly reliable as textbooks.

Work through your study plan. You may want to work alone, or you may find it more helpful to work with a group or with a mentor. Work through the topics and questions provided in chapters 3-6. Be able to define and discuss the topics in your own words rather than memorizing definitions from books. If you are working with a group or mentor, you can also try informal quizzes and questioning techniques.

Proceed to the practice questions. Once you have completed your review, you are ready to benefit from the "Practice Questions" portion of this guide.

Suggestions for using the "Practice Questions" and "Right Answers and Explanations for the Practice Questions" chapters

Read chapter 7 ("Don't Be Defeated by Multiple-Choice Questions"). This chapter will sharpen your skills in reading and answering questions. Succeeding on multiple-choice questions requires careful focus on the question, an eye for detail, and patient sifting of the answer choices.

Answer the practice questions in chapter 8. Make your own test-taking conditions as similar to actual testing conditions as you can. Work on the practice questions in a quiet place without distractions. Remember that the practice questions are only examples of the way the topics are covered in the test. The test you take will have different questions.

Score the practice questions. Go through the detailed answers in chapter 9 ("Right Answers and Explanations") and mark the questions you answered correctly and the ones you missed. Look over the explanations of the questions you missed and see if you understand them.

Decide whether you need more review. After you have looked at your results, decide if there are areas that you need to brush up on before taking the actual test. (The practice questions are grouped by topic, which may help you to spot areas of particular strength or weakness.) Go back to your textbooks and reference materials to see if the topics are covered there. You might also want to go over your questions with a friend or teacher who is familiar with the subject.

Assess your readiness. Do you feel confident about your level of understanding in each of the subject areas? If not, where do you need more work? If you feel ready, complete the checklist in chapter 10 ("Are You Ready?") to double-check that you've thought through the details. If you need more information about registration or the testing situation itself, use the resources in Appendix B: "For More Information."

Chapter 2
Background Information on
The Praxis Series™ Assessments

▶   ▶   ▶   ▶   ▶   ▶   ▶   ▶   ▶   ▶   ▶   ▶

What are The Praxis Series Subject Assessments?

The Praxis Series Subject Assessments are designed by Educational Testing Service (ETS) to assess your knowledge of the subject area you plan to teach, and they are a part of the licensing procedure in many states. This study guide covers an assessment that tests your knowledge of the actual content you hope to be licensed to teach. Your state has adopted The Praxis Series tests because it wants to be certain that you have achieved a specified level of mastery of your subject area before it grants you a license to teach in a classroom.

The Praxis Series tests are part of a national testing program, meaning that the test covered in this study guide is used in more than one state. The advantage of taking Praxis tests is that if you want to move to another state that uses The Praxis Series tests, you can transfer your scores to that state. Passing scores are set by states, however, so if you are planning to apply for licensure in another state, you may find that passing scores are different. You can find passing scores for all states that use The Praxis Series tests in the *Understanding Your Praxis Scores* pamphlet, available in your college's School of Education, online at www.ets.org/praxis, or by calling (800) 772-9476 or (609) 771-7395.

What is Licensure?

Licensure in any area — medicine, law, architecture, accounting, cosmetology — is an assurance to the public that the person holding the license has demonstrated a certain level of competence. The phrase used in licensure is that the person holding the license *will do no harm*. In the case of teacher licensing, a license tells the public that the person holding the license can be trusted to educate children competently and professionally.

Because a license makes such a serious claim about its holder, licensure tests are usually quite demanding. In some fields licensure tests have more than one part and last for more than one day. Candidates for licensure in all fields plan intensive study as part of their professional preparation: some join study groups, others study alone. But preparing to take a licensure test is, in all cases, a professional activity. Because it assesses your entire body of knowledge or skill for the field you want to enter, preparing for a licensure exam takes planning, discipline, and sustained effort. Studying thoroughly is highly recommended.

Why does My State Require The Praxis Series Assessments?

Your state chose The Praxis Series Assessments because the tests assess the breadth and depth of content — called the "domain" of the test — that your state wants its teachers to possess before they begin to teach. The level of content knowledge, reflected in the passing score, is based on recommendations of panels of teachers and teacher educators in each subject area in each state. The state licensing agency and, in some states, the state legislature ratify the passing scores that have been recommended by panels of teachers.

You can find out the passing score required for The Praxis Series Assessments in your state by looking in the pamphlet *Understanding Your Praxis Scores,* which is free from ETS (see above). If you look through this pamphlet, you will see that not all states use the same test modules, and even when they do, the passing scores can differ from state to state.

What kinds of Tests are The Praxis Series Subject Assessments?

Two kinds of tests comprise The Praxis Series Subject Assessments: multiple choice (for which you select your answer from a list of choices) and constructed response (for which you write a response of your own). Multiple-choice tests can survey a wider domain because they can ask more questions in a limited period of time. Constructed-response tests have far fewer questions, but the questions require you to demonstrate the depth of your knowledge in the area covered.

What do the Tests Measure?

The Praxis Series Subject Assessments are tests of content knowledge. They measure your understanding of the subject area you want to teach. The multiple-choice tests measure a broad range of knowledge across your content area. The constructed-response tests measure your ability to explain in depth a few essential topics in your subject area. The content-specific pedagogy tests, most of which are constructed-response, measure your understanding of how to teach certain fundamental concepts in your field. The tests do not measure your actual teaching ability, however. They measure your knowledge of your subject and of how to teach it. The teachers in your field who help us design and write these tests, and the states that require these tests, do so in the belief that knowledge of subject area is the first requirement for licensing. Your teaching ability is a skill that is measured in other ways: observation, videotaped teaching, or portfolios are typically used by states to measure teaching ability. Teaching combines many complex skills, only some of which can be measured by a single test. The Praxis Series Subject Assessments are designed to measure how thoroughly you understand the material in the subject areas in which you want to be licensed to teach.

How were These Tests Developed?

ETS began the development of The Praxis Series Subject Assessments with a survey. For each subject, teachers around the country in various teaching situations were asked to judge which knowledge and skills a beginning teacher in that subject needs to possess. Professors in schools of education who prepare teachers were asked the same questions. These responses were ranked in order of importance and sent out to hundreds of teachers for review. All of the responses to these surveys (called "job analysis surveys") were analyzed to summarize the judgments of these professionals. From their consensus, we developed the specifications for the multiple-choice and constructed-response tests. Each subject area had a committee of practicing teachers and teacher educators who wrote these specifications (guidelines). The specifications were reviewed and eventually approved by teachers. From the test specifications, groups of teachers and professional test developers created test questions.

When your state adopted The Praxis Series Subject Assessments, local panels of practicing teachers and teacher educators in each subject area met to examine the tests question by question and evaluate each question for its relevance to beginning teachers in your state. This is called a "validity study." A test is considered "valid" for a job if it measures what people must know and be able to do on that job. For the test to be adopted in your state, teachers in your state must judge that it is valid.

These teachers and teacher educators also performed a "standard-setting study"; that is, they went through the tests question by question and decided, through a rigorous process, how many questions a beginning teacher would be able to answer correctly. From this study emerged a recommended passing score. The final passing score was approved by your state's licensing agency.

In other words, throughout the development process, practitioners in the teaching field — teachers and teacher educators — have determined what the tests would contain. The practitioners in your state determined which tests would be used for licensure in your subject area and helped decide what score would be needed to achieve licensure. This is how professional licensure works in most fields: those who are already licensed oversee the licensing of new practitioners. When you pass The Praxis Series Subject Assessments, you and the practitioners in your state can be assured that you have the knowledge required to begin practicing your profession.

Chapter 3

Language Arts and Reading: Study Topics

▶   ▶   ▶   ▶   ▶   ▶   ▶   ▶   ▶   ▶   ▶   ▶

Language Arts and Reading: Study Topics

The "Language Arts and Reading" component of the *Elementary Education: Content Knowledge* test covers understanding of literature, text structures and organization, the components of language in writing, literacy acquisition, reading instruction, and communication skills.

The "Language Arts and Reading" section of the test was designed to align with Standard 2b of the *Program Standards for Elementary Teacher Preparation* published by NCATE (National Council for Accreditation of Teacher Education):

> Candidates demonstrate a high level of competence in use of the English language arts and they know, understand, and use concepts from reading, language, and child development to teach reading, writing, speaking, viewing, listening, and thinking skills and to help students successfully apply their developing skills to many different situations, materials, and ideas.

The first three areas in "Language Arts and Reading" — "Understanding Literature," "Text Structures and Organization," and "Language in Writing" — cover basic knowledge. That is, they cover a content-knowledge base that is a foundation for good teaching but not oriented directly toward teaching methods. Many teaching activities depend on this base knowledge (for example, choosing literature for the classroom, helping students understand what they are reading, helping students improve their writing, etc.), but these questions concentrate on the basic knowledge and concepts of language arts, not their pedagogical applications.

The two remaining areas covered in this section — "Literacy Acquisition and Reading Instruction"

and "Communication Skills" — test pedagogical content knowledge. In these questions you are tested on major methods, approaches, concepts, and underlying theories related to assisting children in acquiring literacy, developing students' reading abilities, and enhancing their communication skills.

Using the topic lists that follow: You are not expected to be an expert on all aspects of the topics that follow. But you should understand the major characteristics or aspects of each topic and be able to recognize them in various kinds of examples or selections.

Here, for instance, is one of the topic lists in "Understanding Literature," under "Narratives":

▶ Literary devices and style elements

- Foreshadowing
- Figurative language (e.g., metaphor, simile, hyperbole, personification)
- Symbol
- Imagery
- Word choice
- Mechanics (e.g., punctuation, sentence structure)
- Use of dialect or slang

Referring to textbooks, state standards documents, or other sources as needed, make sure you can describe in your own words what each element or device is. For example, you should be able to think to yourself that "Foreshadowing is an indication or a warning of a future event or action" or "A metaphor is an indirect comparison that vividly describes something by directly identifying it with something else without using 'like' or 'as' (e.g., 'people are books you can read' or 'thoughts follow

Here is an overview of the areas within the "Language Arts and Reading" section:

Understanding Literature
- Narratives
- Nonfiction
- Poetry
- Resource and research material

Text Structures and Organization
- Structural elements in text
- Organizational patterns in text

Language in Writing
- Grammar and usage
- Sentence types and sentence structure
- Orthography and morphology
- Semantics

Content-knowledge base

Literacy Acquisition and Reading Instruction
- Theories and concepts concerning reading development
- Children's literature
- Strategies for word study/solving
- Strategies for comprehension
- Study skills and tools

Communication Skills
- Stages of writing development
- Stages of the writing process
- Spelling development
- Elements of speaking
- Elements of listening

Pedagogical content knowledge

---

winding paths')." It is also very important to be able to recognize each of these elements or devices if it appears in an excerpt of literature.

Special questions marked with stars: Interspersed throughout the topic lists are passages and questions that are preceded by stars (★) and outlined in boxes. These questions show how you might pay attention to particular concepts in preparing for the test. Some of these questions are derived from typical questions children ask, and answering them requires a significant amount of content knowledge. Other questions require you to combine several pieces of knowledge and to formulate an integrated understanding. If you spend time on these examples, you will likely gain increased understanding and a facility with the subject matter covered on the test. You may want to discuss the starred passages, questions, and your answers with a teacher or mentor.

Note that the questions and passages marked with stars are open-ended questions (some with annotated examples), not multiple-choice questions. They are intended as *study* questions not practice questions. Thinking about the answers to an open-ended question will improve your understanding of the fundamental concepts and will probably help you answer a number of related multiple-choice questions.

Understanding Literature

Narratives

Things to study

Be ready to read selections of literature, including children's literature, and answer questions relating to one or more of the topics in this category (e.g., identify how a theme is communicated in a passage, recognize techniques of character development, identify how a setting is established, or evaluate how style elements establish the theme, tone, or mood). You may also be asked definitional or applied questions.

▶ Elements of a story

- Plot elements
  — Rising action
  — Internal and external conflict
  — Complication
  — Suspense
  — Crisis
  — Climax or turning point

- Characterization (through a character's words, thoughts, actions, appearance, etc.)

- Setting (established through description of scenes, colors, smells, etc.)

- Tone

- Theme

- Point of view (first person, third-person objective, third-person omniscient)

- Perspective (attitude of the narrator of the story)

▶ Literary devices and style elements

- Foreshadowing

- Figurative language (e.g., metaphor, simile, hyperbole, personification)

- Symbol

- Imagery

- Word choice

- Mechanics (e.g., punctuation, sentence structure)

- Use of dialect or slang

▶ Fiction genres

- Novel

- Short story

- Science fiction

- Fable

- Myth

- Legend

- Folk tale

- Fairy tale

- Play (comedy, tragedy)

- Mystery

- Historical fiction

- Adventure story

- Fantasy

★ Read the following fiction selection, from Toni Cade Bambara's "The War of the Wall." What is the most important perspective? How is it communicated? What is the theme? What stylistic elements do you recognize?

Me and Lou had no time for courtesies. We were late for school. So we just flat out told the painter lady to quit messing with the wall. It was our wall, and she had no right coming into our neighborhood painting on it. Stirring in the paint bucket and not even looking at us, she mumbled something about Mr. Eubanks, the barber, giving her permission. That had nothing to do with it as far as we were concerned. We've been pitching pennies against that wall since we were little kids. Old folks have been dragging their chairs out to sit in the shade of the wall for years. Big kids have been playing handball against the wall since so-called integration when the crazies 'cross town poured cement in our pool so we couldn't use it. I'd sprained my neck one time boosting my cousin Lou up to chisel Jimmy Lyons's name into the wall when we found out he was never coming home from the war in Vietnam to take us fishing.

First-person point of view. Using the wrong pronoun ("Me" instead of "I") immediately establishes a narrator who makes grammatical mistakes but is untroubled by them and speaks quickly and colloquially.

Use of slang ("flat out," "messing with the wall," and "crazies 'cross town")

Reflects the narrator's perspective of bitterness toward the woman: he suggests that she's avoiding his glance and has no good excuse for being there.

Getting to the theme: the wall has been vital to the community. Structurally, the paragraph builds up to the important act of the writing of the name of Jimmy Lyons — the memorializing of a friend of the kids in the neighborhood who died in Vietnam.

★ This box highlights some of the elements that you would be expected to pay attention to:

Me and Lou had no time for courtesies. We were late for school. So we just flat out told the painter lady to quit messing with the wall. It was our wall, and she had no right coming into our neighborhood painting on it. Stirring in the paint bucket and not even looking at us, she mumbled something about Mr. Eubanks, the barber, giving her permission. That had nothing to do with it as far as we were concerned. We've been pitching pennies against that wall since we were little kids. Old folks have been dragging their chairs out to sit in the shade of the wall for years. Big kids have been playing handball against the wall since so-called integration when the crazies 'cross town poured cement in our pool so we couldn't use it. I'd sprained my neck one time boosting my cousin Lou up to chisel Jimmy Lyons's name into the wall when we found out he was never coming home from the war in Vietnam to take us fishing.

Angry tone; the narrator is angry at the woman.

Nonfiction

Things to study

Be ready to read selections of nonfiction and answer questions relating to one or more of the topics in this category. You may also be asked definitional or applied questions.

▶ Comprehension of nonfiction

- Identify the main idea, primary hypothesis, or primary purpose (e.g., to persuade, to inform, to analyze, or to evaluate)

- Evaluate the clarity of the information

- Identify the author's point of view or perspective

- Make valid inferences or conclusions based on the selection

- Identify, where appropriate, an author's appeal to reason, appeal to emotion, or appeal to authority

- Evaluate the relationship between stated generalizations and actual evidence given

- Evaluate the organization of a selection

- For informational texts, evaluate the effectiveness of their organizational and graphic aids

▶ Nonfiction genres

- Biography

- Autobiography

- Essay

- News article

- Editorial

- Professional journal article

- Book on a research topic or other issue

- Book review

- Political speech

- Technical manual

- Primary source material

★ Read the following nonfiction selection, from Esther Rudomin Hautzig's *The Endless Steppe: Growing Up in Siberia.* What genre is it from? What is its overall purpose? Are there any figures of speech that help to illustrate the key points? How does the author make a comment on economic differences in her society?

The spring came, the rather thin spring of the Siberian steppe. But it is impossible to have any thoughts of the thin Siberian spring without first recalling the thick mud. What with the spring rains and the thaw, the steppe became an ocean of mud, and to walk through it was like walking through knee-deep molasses. If you were not lucky enough to own a pair of *sapogy,* the handsome knee-high leather boots that the well-to-do wore, if you had nothing but the same old pair of school oxfords, or even *pimy* boots, along with the energy needed to pull a foot up from the bottom of this mud, you also more often than not had to stop to hunt for the shoe left behind. Whatever you wore, the object developed a crust of mud that had to be broken off after each excursion. While I may have found some of this fun, my mother did not; her trips to and from the bakery in the mud required more energy than she had.

The main purpose of this selection is to relate a personal memory of the distinctiveness of Siberian mud in the spring.

An observation focusing on differences between the experiences of the rich and the poor and how they were evident in the shoes people wore.

First-person point of view. Reflection on a personal memory suggests that the passage is most likely from a memoir.

★This box highlights some of the elements that you would be expected to pay attention to.

The spring came, the rather thin spring of the Siberian steppe. But it is impossible to have any thoughts of the thin Siberian spring without first recalling the thick mud. What with the spring rains and the thaw, the steppe became an ocean of mud, and to walk through it was like walking through knee-deep molasses. If you were not lucky enough to own a pair of *sapogy*, the handsome knee-high leather boots that the well-to-do wore, if you had nothing but the same old pair of school oxfords, or even *pimy* boots, along with the energy needed to pull a foot up from the bottom of this mud, you also more often than not had to stop to hunt for the shoe left behind. Whatever you wore, the object developed a crust of mud that had to be broken off after each excursion. While I may have found some of this fun, my mother did not; her trips to and from the bakery in the mud required more energy than she had.

Metaphor

Simile

Poetry

Things to study

Be ready to read one or more poems and answer questions relating to one or more of the topics in this category. You may also be asked definitional or applied questions.

▶ Construction of meaning in poetry

- Main idea or theme
- Symbolism
- Tone, emotion

▶ Poetic elements

- Verse
  — Meter
  — Stanza
  — Line length
  — Punctuation

- Rhyme and sound patterns
  — Rhyme scheme
  — Onomatopoeia
  — Repetition of words
  — Alliteration
  — Assonance

- Imagery and figures of speech
  — Image
  — Personification
  — Metaphor
  — Simile
  — Hyperbole

▶ Poetic types and forms

- Lyrical
- Concrete
- Free verse
- Narrative
- Couplet
- Elegy
- Sonnet
- Limerick
- Haiku

★ Read the following selection from Alfred Noyes' poem "The Highwayman." What rhyme and meter patterns are present? How is it organized? Is it a narrative poem? What kinds of sounds and imagery appear in the poem? What is the tone or emotion? What is the poem's main focus?

The wind was a torrent of darkness among the gusty trees,

The moon was a ghostly galleon tossed upon cloudy seas,

The road was a ribbon of moonlight over the purple moor,

And the highwayman came riding-

 Riding-riding-

The highwayman came riding, up to the old inn door.

He'd a French cocked hat on his forehead, a bunch of lace

 at his chin,

A coat of the claret velvet, and breeches of brown doeskin.

They fitted with never a wrinkle. His boots were up to the thigh.

And he rode with a jeweled twinkle.

 His pistol butts a-twinkle.

His rapier hilt a-twinkle, under the jeweled sky.

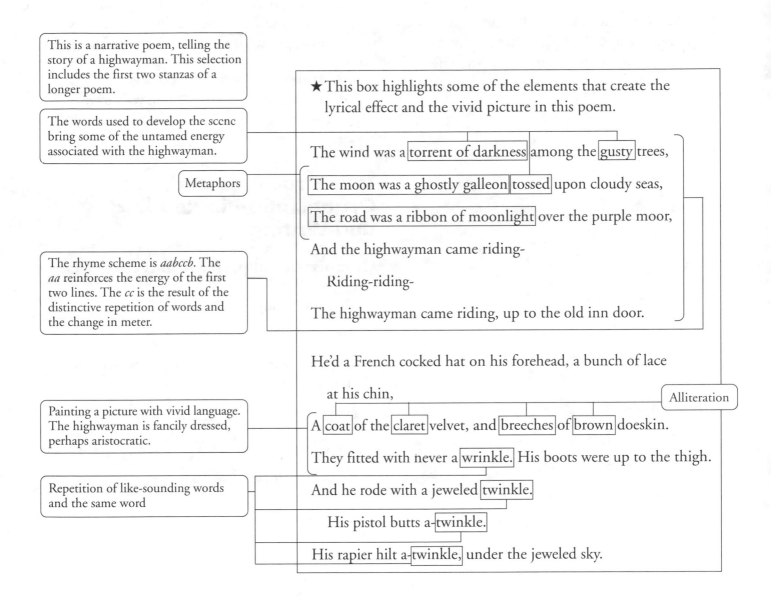

This is a narrative poem, telling the story of a highwayman. This selection includes the first two stanzas of a longer poem.

The words used to develop the scene bring some of the untamed energy associated with the highwayman.

Metaphors

The rhyme scheme is *aabccb*. The *aa* reinforces the energy of the first two lines. The *cc* is the result of the distinctive repetition of words and the change in meter.

Painting a picture with vivid language. The highwayman is fancily dressed, perhaps aristocratic.

Repetition of like-sounding words and the same word

★ This box highlights some of the elements that create the lyrical effect and the vivid picture in this poem.

The wind was a torrent of darkness among the gusty trees,

The moon was a ghostly galleon tossed upon cloudy seas,

The road was a ribbon of moonlight over the purple moor,

And the highwayman came riding-

    Riding-riding-

The highwayman came riding, up to the old inn door.

He'd a French cocked hat on his forehead, a bunch of lace

    at his chin,

Alliteration

A coat of the claret velvet, and breeches of brown doeskin.

They fitted with never a wrinkle. His boots were up to the thigh.

And he rode with a jeweled twinkle.

    His pistol butts a-twinkle.

His rapier hilt a-twinkle, under the jeweled sky.

Resource and research material

Things to study

Questions will address both appropriateness of resource material for particular tasks and recognition of what these sources can offer.

▶ Reference works
- Dictionary
- Encyclopedia
- Thesaurus
- Atlas
- Almanac

▶ Internet
- Keyword search
- Databases
- Bulletin boards

▶ Other sources
- Books
- Newspapers and magazines
- Professional journals
- *Reader's Guide to Periodical Literature*
- Primary sources, including reproductions of original documents

▶ Using resources and reference material
- Appropriateness of various sources to the project
- Quotations and paraphrases of experts
- Footnotes
- Bibliography

★ For a project about the painting techniques of Vincent van Gogh for upper elementary students, what are the top three kinds of resources you would recommend to the students and why?

★ What about for a project about a political demonstration that happened in your town or city ten years ago?

Text Structures and Organization in Reading and Writing

Organizational patterns in text

Things to study

Short excerpts will be given, accompanied by questions asking for recognition of one or more of these patterns.

▶ Patterns of expository writing
- Compare and contrast
- Chronological sequence
- Spatial sequence
- Cause and effect
- Problem and solution

Structural elements in text

Things to study

Single sentences or short excerpts will be given, accompanied by questions asking for recognition of one or more particular elements.

▶ Thesis statement

▶ Conclusion statement

▶ Transition words and phrases

▶ Supporting the thesis with the use of

- Examples

- Quotations

- Paraphrases of experts' statements

- Summaries of information found in research sources

- Analogies

▶ Approaching one's topic with the purpose of

- Criticizing

- Analyzing

- Evaluating pros and cons

★ In the following passage, identify

- the thesis statement
- a sentence in the passive voice
- a transitional word or phrase

The only real innovation during the Renaissance period in terms of transport was seen in the Americas. By the fifteenth century, the Incas had constructed a network of fine roads for couriers. Rivers were crossed by monkey bridges of cables of plaited agave fibre, or floating bridges, or pontoons of reeds. In addition, the Incas used caravans of llamas, bred as beasts of burden even though they could only carry a hundredweight, and could only travel fifteen miles a day. These were the only important domestic animals of the Americas before 1492, and they were quite inadequate.

Language in Writing

Grammar and usage

Things to study

Single sentences will be given, accompanied by questions asking you to recognize particular elements or errors. You may also be asked definitional questions about these topics.

▶ Parts of speech

- Noun: proper, common, collective

- Pronoun

- Verb

- Adjective

- Adverb

- Preposition
- Conjunction
- Phrase
  — Participial phrase
  — Prepositional phrase
  — Appositive phrase
- Clause
  — Independent clause
  — Dependent clause
- ▶ Syntactical systems
- Subject-verb agreement
- Verb tenses: present, past, present perfect, past perfect, future, and future perfect
- Voice of verb: active or passive
- Pronoun-antecedent agreement and weak reference
- Correct use of infinitive and participle

Sentence types and sentence structure

Things to study

Single sentences will be given, accompanied by questions asking you to identify types or structures, or to correct errors. You may also be asked definitional questions about these topics.

- ▶ Sentence types
- Declarative
- Interrogative
- Exclamatory
- Imperative
- ▶ Sentence structure
- Simple
- Compound

- Complex
- Compound-complex
- Sentence fragment

Orthography and morphology

Things to study

Word or sentence examples will be given, accompanied by questions asking you to identify key orthographical or morphological elements

- ▶ Affixes: prefix, suffix
- ▶ Roots
- ▶ Inflectional endings
- ▶ Clusters (combining clusters to make compound words)

Semantics

Things to study

Word or sentence examples will be given, accompanied by questions asking you to sort through the semantic problem presented. You may also be asked definitional questions about these topics.

- ▶ Homonyms
- ▶ Antonyms
- ▶ Synonyms
- ▶ Multiple-meaning words
- ▶ Words used figuratively or idiomatically (e.g., he "wolfed" down his food)
- ▶ Meaning-shifts due to alternative word order or punctuation

Literacy Acquisition and Reading Instruction

Theories and concepts concerning reading development

Things to study

Questions will address major characteristics of these concepts and approaches.

▶ Major elements of the emergent literacy theory and major conclusions of recent research

▶ Factors influencing the development of emergent reading

- Concepts about print
- Sight vocabulary
- Phonemic awareness
- Alphabetic principle
- Social interaction (support by adults and peers)
- Frequent experiences with print
- Prior knowledge (schema)
- Motivation
- Fluency

▶ Experiences that support emergent readers

- Direct instruction
- Social interaction
- Shared reading
- Repeated readings
- Reader response

- Word walls
- Text innovation (rewrites)
- Shared writing

★ What are some of the major relationships between and among reading, writing, speaking, listening, and viewing, and why are these relationships important for teachers of emergent readers to understand?

Children's literature

Things to study

School or classroom situations related to the topics below will be given, accompanied by questions asking about important criteria, priorities, or decisions.

▶ Selection of materials

- Who selects and in what situations?
- Quality of material
- Appropriate content
- Needs and interests of children
- School curriculum
- Balance in the collection

▶ Traditional criteria for evaluating fiction — plot, character, theme

▶ Specialized criteria for these types of literature

- Picture books
- Poetry
- Informational books
- Biography

◗ Additional criteria for these genres of fiction

- Realistic story
- Modern fantasy
- Historical fiction
- Mystery

★ Choosing a poem that features a repeated refrain for reading aloud to kindergarten students is a good example of using the criterion of the children's enjoyment for selecting literature. What are some other examples of selection criteria you would need to use when choosing literature to read aloud to kindergarten students?

Strategies for word study/solving

Things to study

Student examples will be given, accompanied by questions asking about cue-related issues. You may also be asked definitional questions about these topics.

◗ Cues and how students use them

- Context: semantic and syntactic systems
- Phonological system and visual information
  — Relationship to print
  — Recognizing whole words
  — Word patterns
  — Syllables
  — Letters in sequence

★ An informal reading inventory is shown below: the text from the printed book is shown below in regular print; above it, in italics, are shown the words that deviated from the printed text when a particular fourth-grade student was asked to read the text aloud. What do the student's miscues indicate? Is there a need for instruction in the syntactic system? Is the student attending sufficiently to making meaning? How is the student using phonics knowledge?

Samuel and his cousin John Adams felt the

indenture
same way about America's independence. Yet

operations   racing
they had different opinions about riding horses.

John thought that Samuel should ride a horse

agreed
like other men did. Samuel argued that walking

cannon
or riding in a carriage suited him better.

Strategies for comprehension

Things to study

Classroom situations related to the topics below will be given, accompanied by questions asking about most appropriate strategies. You may also be asked definitional questions about these topics.

◗ Use of prior knowledge

◗ Retelling

◗ Guided reading

◗ Fluency

◗ Reader response

◆ Comprehension as a strategic process

- Solving words
- Adjusting reading according to purpose and context
- Metacognition
- Maintaining fluency
- Making connections (personal, world, text)

★ A class is reading a book that has chapter numbers but no chapter titles. The teacher asks the students to think of an appropriate title for each chapter. What is the main purpose in choosing this activity? Why is it a useful activity?

Study skills and tools

Things to study

Examples of assignments will be given, accompanied by questions asking about most appropriate strategies. You may also be asked definitional questions about these topics.

◆ SQ3R

◆ KWL

◆ Note taking

◆ Marking and coding

◆ Graphic organizers

★ What are some effective ways to use graphic organizers if students understand most of the details in a unit, but not the central idea of the unit?

◆ Finding information in charts, tables, graphs

★ What are some effective ways of guiding students to understand articles that feature text and a variety of graphics?

Communication Skills

Stages of writing development

Things to study

Student examples or typical situations or assignments will be presented, accompanied by questions asking about a particular phase of writing. You may also be asked definitional questions about these topics.

◆ Phases

- Picture writing
- Scribble writing
- Random letter
- Invented spelling
- Conventional writing

◆ Concurrent development with reading

★ Here are three examples of student writing. Into which of the "phases" listed on the previous page would you put each one, and why?

Example 1

Example 2

My Kusun ApRIL came to play With me She playd BasBol

Example 3

AKTPS

Stages of the writing process

Things to study

Examples or situations will be given, accompanied by questions asking about most appropriate strategies and decisions.

▶ Recursive nature of the process

- Explore/Prewrite
- Draft
- Edit
- Publish

Spelling development

Things to study

Student examples or typical situations or assignments will be presented, accompanied by questions asking about a particular stage of spelling. You may also be asked definitional questions about these topics.

▶ Constructive nature of the development stages
— Scribble
— Prephonemic
— Early phonemic
— Letter name
— Transitional
— Derivational
— Conventional

★Here are three sets of examples of student spelling. Into which of the "stages" listed above does each row fit, and why?

Student 1

SRY	Lvh	yeB	ls	Be
fish	bend	jumped	shove	witch

Student 2

7ss	nd	Jd	hd	Ws
fish	bend	jumped	shove	witch

Student 3

sailer	provion	spashal	slowed	flatt
sailor	prison	special	slowed	flat

Elements of speaking

Things to study

Questions will ask about important concepts related to one or more of the following elements, especially as applicable to instructional elements or activities.

- Purpose
- Audience
- Inclusion of visuals
- Tone
- Opening and closing
- Details and anecdotes
- Volume, pitch, pace, gestures
- Eye contact
- Voice modulation
- Focus, organization, structure, point of view

Elements of listening

Things to study

Questions will ask about important concepts related to one or more of the following elements, especially as applicable to instructional elements or activities.

- Listening to and following directions
- Responding to questions
- Responding to literature read aloud
- Agreeing or disagreeing with the ideas in a speech
- Asking for clarification
- Expanding on an idea
- Repeating or paraphrasing to verify one's understanding
- Calling for evidence
- Summarizing major ideas and supporting evidence
- Interpreting volume, pitch, pace, gestures
- Evaluating mood or tone

Chapter 4
Mathematics: Study Topics

▶   ▶   ▶   ▶   ▶   ▶   ▶   ▶   ▶   ▶   ▶   ▶

Mathematics: Study Topics

The "Mathematics" component of the *Elementary Education: Content Knowledge* test covers understanding of basic mathematical concepts and operations, the ability to solve problems using basic algebra, geometry, probability, and statistics, and the ability to read and interpret data presented in various kinds of charts and graphs. Mathematical reasoning and problem-solving skills underlie many of the questions in this section of the test.

The "Mathematics" section of the test was designed to align with Standard 2d of the *Program Standards for Elementary Teacher Preparation* published by NCATE (National Council for Accreditation of Teacher Education):

> Candidates know, understand, and use the major concepts, procedures, and reasoning processes of mathematics that define number systems and number sense, geometry, measurement, statistics and probability, and algebra in order to foster student understanding.

The emphasis in this section of the test is on understanding fundamental concepts, the ability to reason logically, and the ability to use mathematical techniques in problem-solving. The emphasis is *not* on calculating numbers in your head or on paper — in fact, you are allowed to use a basic four-function calculator in the test center, and it is recommended that you use a calculator when you work through the practice questions.

Using the topic lists that follow: You are not expected to be an expert on all the topics that follow. But you should be able to understand and apply the topics. For example, here is one of the topic lists in "Number Systems and Number Sense," under "Standard algorithms for the four basic operations":

- ▶ Commutative, associative, and distributive properties

- ▶ Order of operations — the basic rules about what operation is done before others in equations such as $3 \times 6 + 7$, $5(3 + 12) + 42(23 - 4)$, and $\dfrac{4(12 - 3)}{6 - 3}$

- ▶ Modeling operations — using a grid or number line or groups of objects to show how to add or multiply numbers

Using textbooks, state standards documents, and other sources as needed, make sure you can describe in your own words what, for example, the "commutative property" is. And then be sure you can apply it in a typical real-world problem. For "order of operations," you will need to find in a textbook or other source the basic rules governing the sequence of operations, then test yourself on the rules by figuring out the order of operations in several typical equations. In "modeling operations," think about how you could demonstrate addition on a number line, or how you could demonstrate simple multiplication using groups of objects.

Special questions marked with stars:
Interspersed throughout the topic lists are questions that are preceded by stars (★) and outlined in boxes. These questions show how you might pay attention to particular concepts in preparing for the test. Some of these questions are derived from typical questions children ask, and answering them usually requires a significant amount of content knowledge. Other questions require you to combine several pieces of knowledge and formulate an integrated understanding. If you spend time on these questions, you will likely gain increased understanding and a facility with the subject matter covered on the test. You may want

Here is an overview of the areas within the "Mathematics" section:

Number Systems and Number Sense ——————
- Meaning and use of numbers
- Standard algorithms for the four basic operations
- Appropriate computation strategies and reasonableness of results
- Methods of mathematical investigation

Algebraic Concepts ——————
- Basic algebraic methods and representations
- Additive and multiplicative inverses
- The special properties of zero and one
- Equalities and inequalities
- Patterns
- Algebraic formulas

Informal Geometry and Measurement ——————
- Properties and relationships in figures and shapes in two and three dimensions
- Angles and the Pythagorean theorem
- Transformations
- Geometric models
- Nets
- Standard units of measurement

Data Organization and Interpretation ——————
- Visual displays of quantitative information
- Simple probability
- Outcomes and events
- Statistics

to discuss these questions and your answers with a teacher or mentor.

Note that the questions marked with stars are open-ended, not multiple-choice. They are intended as *study* questions, not practice questions. Thinking about the answers to an open-ended question will improve your understanding of fundamental concepts and will probably help you answer a number of related multiple-choice questions. For example, if you answer and think about the following starred question:

> ★ Why is it that 3 is greater than 2, but $\frac{1}{3}$ is less than $\frac{1}{2}$?

you have probably prepared yourself to answer the following multiple-choice question:

Which of the following numbers is *least*?

(A) $\frac{1}{7}$ (B) $\frac{11}{70}$ (C) $\frac{101}{700}$ (D) $\frac{1,001}{7,000}$

(The correct answer is (A).)

Number Systems and Number Sense

Meaning and use of numbers

Things to study

▶ Be able to recognize examples of pre-numeration activities in which children classify objects, look for patterns among objects, or put objects into sets.

▶ Be able to answer questions about or apply these concepts.

- How numbers are named, place value, and order of magnitude of numbers (e.g., recognize that 100 is 1,000 times 0.1, or that .002 is $\frac{2}{1,000}$)

- Cardinal number (e.g., 5 people)

- Ordinal number (e.g., the 5th person in line)

- "Base 10" and what a "base" system is

- Recognize correct order (e.g., least and greatest) among whole numbers, fractions, and decimals (e.g., recognize that $-3 < -2$, or that $\frac{1}{2}$ is between $\frac{1}{3}$ and $\frac{2}{3}$, or that 1.9 is closer to 2 than to 1)

> ★ Why is it that 3 is greater than 2, but $\frac{1}{3}$ is less than $\frac{1}{2}$?

- Scientific notation: using powers of 10 (e.g., 10^4) to express large numbers (e.g., 43,700 is written in scientific notation as 4.37×10^4)

> ★ Is the square of a number always greater than the number? Consider numbers such as 3, -2, $\frac{1}{4}$, and 0.

- Set properties (e.g., elements in a set, union, intersection, complementation)

▶ Number terminology: Be able to answer questions about or apply these concepts.

- Prime number

> ★ Are 1 and 2 prime numbers? Why or why not?

- Composite number

- Greatest common factor

- Least common multiple

- Equivalent forms of numbers; i.e., a number can be represented in more than one way (e.g., 0.5 is equivalent to $\frac{1}{2}$ and 50%)

- Even number

- Odd number

> ★ Is zero an even number or an odd number?
>
> ★ Is the sum of two even numbers always even? What about the sum of two odd numbers?

- Remainder (e.g., 27 divided by 12 equals 2 with a remainder of 3)

- Factor tree; i.e., showing the prime factors of a number in a simple diagram

> ★ Make a factor tree for 60.

Standard algorithms for the four basic operations

Things to study

Be able to answer questions about or apply these concepts.

▶ Commutative, associative, and distributive properties

▶ Order of operations — the basic rules about what operation is done before others in equations such as $3 \times 6 + 7$,

$5(3 + 12) + 42(23 - 4)$, and $\dfrac{4(12 - 3)}{6 - 3}$

$5 \times 15 \quad + \quad 42 \times 19$

▶ Modeling operations — using a grid or number line or groups of objects to show how to add or multiply numbers

---

★ Why do we put an arrow on the end of a number line?

★ Create two or three different ways of visually representing the product of 2 and 4. Think of objects that elementary students would relate to.

A number of questions on the test will involve real-world problem solving with whole numbers, fractions, decimals, integers, percents, ratios, rates, and scales.

▶ Some applied problems involve percent, so make sure you are comfortable working with problems of this type.

★ If a movie ticket was $5 last week and this week is $6, what was the percent increase?

▶ Some applied problems involve ratio, so make sure you are comfortable working with problems of this type.

★ If the scale used on a blueprint is 1 inch to 4 feet and the drawing of a room is 4.5 inches wide, how wide is the room?

Appropriate computation strategies and reasonableness of results

Things to study

▶ Be able to recognize the various methods for computing with numbers (calculator, paper and pencil, mental computation, rounding up or down, estimating) and be able to choose the most appropriate strategy for a given situation (e.g., using a calculator is best for multiplying three or more large numbers; mental computation is best for quickly adding pairs of small numbers).

▶ Be able to estimate the result of a calculation and determine the reasonableness of an estimate (e.g., recognize that 34×987 is close to $34 \times 1,000$).

★ Is 60 kilograms a reasonable weight for a 6-year-old child? Explain by using a benchmark for a kilogram (i.e., an easy-to-manipulate translation to pounds).

Methods of mathematical investigation

Things to study

▶ Be able to recognize the various strategies for solving mathematical problems (e.g., drawing a picture, working backwards, finding a pattern, adding lines to a geometric figure) and be able to choose the most appropriate strategy for a given problem.

> ★ Write a problem that uses the "working backwards" method. Be sure to give the end result from which to work.

Algebraic Concepts

Basic algebraic methods and representations

Things to study

Be able to answer questions about or apply these concepts.

▶ Variable: Be able to translate a verbal expression into one involving a variable.

> ★ How would you translate the following statement into a mathematical expression that includes variables? "The number of girls is 3 more than the number of boys."

▶ Expression

▶ Algebraic equation: Be able to write and solve algebraic equations.

> ★ In the example above, if there are 41 students, how many are girls?
>
> ★ What is the difference between an expression and an equation?

▶ The xy-coordinate system and why it is important

Additive and multiplicative inverses

Things to study

Be able to answer questions about or apply these concepts.

▶ The negative of a number (e.g., the negative of 3 is -3, and the negative of the expression $x - 3$ is $3 - x$)

▶ The sum of a number and its negative

▶ The reciprocal of a number (e.g., the reciprocal of 3 is $\frac{1}{3}$)

▶ The product of a number and its reciprocal

The special properties of zero and one

Things to study

Be able to answer questions about or apply these concepts.

▶ The product of any number and zero

▶ Zero divided by any number

- Any number divided by zero

★ Why is $\frac{0}{1}$ equal to 0, but $\frac{1}{0}$ not ? Consider using $\frac{20}{5} = 4$ and relating it to $20 = 5 \times 4$ to explain this oddity.

- The meaning of x to the zero power

Equalities and inequalities

Things to study

Be able to answer questions about or apply the symbols <, >, and = and explain what they mean.

Patterns

Things to study

Be able to answer questions about or apply the concept of patterns, including patterns that can be found in

- An array of integers
- An algorithm
- Pascal's triangle
- A sequence of numbers
- Geometric figures

Algebraic formulas

Things to study

Be able to

- Substitute different values into a formula
- Interpret a formula graphically
- Transform a formula (e.g., solve $C = \frac{5}{9}(F - 32)$ for F)

Informal Geometry and Measurement

Properties and relationships in figures and shapes in two and three dimensions

Things to study

Be able to answer questions about or apply these concepts.

- How to compute the area of a rectangle or a triangle
- How to compute the area of a circle
- How to compute the circumference of a circle
- How to compute volume (or capacity)
- How to compute perimeter

★ Do rectangles that have the same perimeter always have the same area?

★ For a given perimeter, what is the shape with the greatest area?

- Parallelism and what it means when we say two lines are parallel
- Perpendicularity and what it means when we say two lines are perpendicular
- The basic properties of all squares
- The basic properties of all circles
- The basic properties of all cubes
- The basic properties of all spheres
- The basic properties of all rectangles

★ If a figure is a rectangle, is it also a square?

If a figure is a square, is it also a rectangle?

A number of the questions on the test will require knowledge of the properties and relationships above to solve measurement and spatial word problems.

▶ Some problems will involve finding the area measurement of odd shapes.

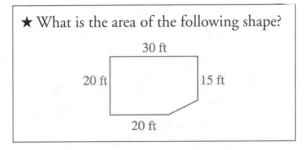

★ What is the area of the following shape?

30 ft

20 ft   15 ft

20 ft

▶ Some problems will involve finding the volume of cylinders and other three-dimensional shapes.

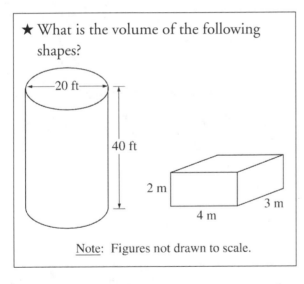

★ What is the volume of the following shapes?

20 ft

40 ft

2 m

4 m   3 m

Note: Figures not drawn to scale.

▶ Some problems will require you to recognize symmetrical designs and use the recognition to answer questions about area or volume.

★ Consider a pair of gloves. Do they have mirror symmetry when considered as two-dimensional objects? From the perspective of three-dimensional symmetry, explain why you can't fit a left-hand glove on your right hand.

▶ Some problems will require you to recognize relationships of figures and shapes (e.g., a triangle made up of two smaller triangles) and use the recognition to answer relationships about perimeter, area, and angles.

★ Draw a trapezoid that can be subdivided into four congruent right triangles.

★ Draw a trapezoid that can be subdivided into three equilateral triangles.

Angles and the Pythagorean theorem

Things to study

Be able to answer questions about or apply these concepts.

▶ How angles are measured

▶ Right angle

▶ The relationship between the three angles in a triangle

▶ Isosceles triangle

▶ Right triangle

★ Can a right triangle be isosceles?

▶ Hypotenuse

▶ The use of the Pythagorean theorem

Transformations

Things to study

Be able to answer questions about or apply these concepts.

▶ The major kinds of transformation are shown below.

Rotation (turn)   **Reflection (flip)**   **Slide**

★ What stays the same when a transformation is applied?

★ What changes when a transformation is applied?

★ Describe the transformation shown below. What stays the same and what changes?

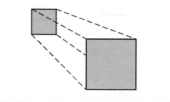

Geometric models

Things to study

These skills may help you solve problems on the test. These are more advanced than most of the other topics, so you may need to get help.

▶ Making a geometric model of an arithmetic operation

★ On a number line, draw arrows to model this calculation: $16 - 8 + 4 - 2$

★ On a grid, model 24 as a product of integers in four different ways.

▶ Making a geometric model of an algebraic factorization

★ On a grid, model 24 as the product of mixed numbers or decimals.

★ On a grid, model 24 as the product of numbers that contain square roots.

▶ Making a geometric model of the sum of a series

★ $\dfrac{1}{2} + \dfrac{1}{4} + \dfrac{1}{8} + \ldots$ is an infinite sequence. Use a square to show that the sum of the sequence is 1. Hint — start this way:

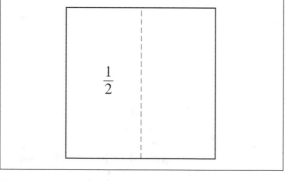

Nets

Things to study

This skill may help you solve problems on the test.

▶ Reorganizing a three-dimensional shape into a two-dimensional shape, e.g., the "net" of the three-dimensional cube below is the two-dimensional shape to its right.

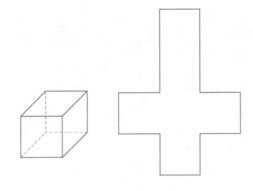

> ★ How could you estimate the surface area of a soup can using a net of the can made from graph paper?

Standard units of measurement

Things to study

Be able to answer questions about or apply these concepts.

▶ Time measurements and calculations in hours and minutes

> ★ What natural phenomena are the basis for many of our time measurements?

▶ English measurement system (inches, feet, yards, miles, pint, quart, gallon, ounce, pound, ton, degree [Fahrenheit])

▶ Metric system (meters, liters, grams, degree [Celsius]) (prefixes *milli-, centi-, kilo-*)

> ★ Name some countries where the English system is used and some countries where the metric system is used.

▶ Converting from one unit to another in the same system

▶ Solving real-world problems using these units of measurement

▶ Reading scales with various gradations

Data Organization and Interpretation

Visual displays of quantitative information

Things to study

One or more questions on the test will require you to read and interpret data in one or more of the following formats.

▶ Bar graph

▶ Line graph

▶ Circle graph

> ★ Can a circle graph and a line graph display the same information? Why or why not?

Pictograph

Table

Stem-and-leaf plot

> ★ How is a stem-and-leaf plot like a bar graph? How is it different?

Scatterplot

Frequency table

Histogram

Venn diagram

One or more questions on the test will require you to recognize relationships in data in visual displays and perform one or more of the following.

Determine an average

Determine a weighted average

Determine a range

Find the median

Find the mode

> ★ Describe a real-life use of a mode.

One or more questions on the test will require you to recognize trends and patterns in a visual display and perform one or more of the following.

Observe groupings

Make comparisons

Make predictions or extrapolations

◆ Recognize direct or inverse relationships

> ★ Describe a real-life situation that illustrates a direct, proportional relationship.
>
> ★ Describe a real-life situation that illustrates a direct, inverse-proportional relationship.

Simple probability

Things to study

Be able to answer questions about or apply these concepts.

◆ Probability

◆ How simple probability is calculated

◆ Models that can be used to illustrate probability concepts, e.g., spinners, number cubes, balls in a jar

Outcomes and events

Things to study

Be able to answer questions about or apply these concepts.

◆ The number of ways an event can happen, e.g., a coin toss can happen two ways, a number cube can happen 6 ways, two number cubes can happen 36 ways: $6 \times 6 = 36$

◆ Sample spaces and counting techniques: defining and counting all possible outcomes

> ★ Make a sample space for the possible outcomes of the toss of three fair coins. Explain why the computation $2 \times 2 \times 2$ gives the number of points in the sample space.

◗ Tree diagrams: illustrating all ways for an event to happen

◗ Combinations: counting when order does *not* matter

◗ Permutations: counting when order does matter

Statistics

Things to study

Be able to answer questions about or apply these concepts.

◗ Average (arithmetic mean) and how it is calculated

> ★ Is the average of two different numbers ever greater than one of them?
>
> ★ Can I find the average of 10 numbers if I know the sum of them but not the numbers themselves?

◗ Median and how is it identified

> ★ Can I find the median of 10 numbers if I know the sum of them but not the numbers themselves?

◗ Mode and how is it identified

◗ Range

◗ Spread

Chapter 5
Social Studies: Study Topics

▶ ▶ ▶ ▶ ▶ ▶ ▶ ▶ ▶ ▶ ▶ ▶ ▶

Social Studies: Study Topics

The "Social Studies" component of the *Elementary Education: Content Knowledge* test covers geography, world history, United States history, political science, economics, anthropology, sociology, and psychology.

The "Social Studies" section of the test was designed to align with Standard 2e of the *Program Standards for Elementary Teacher Preparation* published by NCATE (National Council for Accreditation of Teacher Education):

> Candidates know, understand, and use the major concepts and modes of inquiry from the social studies — the integrated study of history, geography, the social sciences, and other related areas — to promote elementary students' abilities to make informed decisions as citizens of a culturally diverse democratic society and interdependent world. The social studies include history, geography, the social sciences (such as anthropology, archaeology, economics, political science, psychology, and sociology).

The "Social Studies" component of the test focuses on understanding important social, economic, cultural and political concepts, geographical thinking, the workings of governmental systems, important historical events, and contributions of notable individuals within their historical and cultural context. The areas within social studies are mutually enriching and interdependent, and many of the questions on the test will require knowledge and integration of two or more areas.

Note that most states' standards for kindergarten through grade 12 learning include standards that address individual state histories. Since this test, like almost all of The Praxis Series Subject Assessments, are used in a number of states, there are no specific state history questions.

Using the topic lists that follow: You are not expected to be an expert on the topics that follow. But you should understand the major characteristics or aspects of each topic and be able to relate the topic to various situations presented in the test questions, e.g., a map, picture, graph, table, quotation. For instance, here is one of the topic lists in "World History," under "Non-European civilizations":

▶ Islamic civilizations

- Origins, beliefs, and the spread of Islam

- Theological and cultural differences from other belief systems

- Present-day locations of largest populations of Islamic people

Using textbooks, state standards documents, and other sources as needed, make sure you can describe in your own words a brief history of Islam's origins and spread as well as the main theological and cultural differences from other belief systems. Find materials that will help you identify the present-day locations of Islamic people. On the test you may be asked direct questions on one or more of these topics, or you may be asked to connect an aspect of Islam's history with a map, a picture, a quotation, or a comparison with another culture.

Special questions marked with stars: Interspersed throughout the topic lists are questions that are preceded by stars (★) and outlined in boxes. These questions show how you might pay attention to particular concepts in preparing for the test. Some of these questions are derived from typical questions children ask, and answering them requires a significant amount of content knowledge. Other

Here is an overview of the areas within the "Social Studies" section:

Geography

- The world in spatial terms
- Places and regions
- Physical systems
- Human systems
- Environment and society
- Uses of geography

World History

- Prehistory and early civilizations
- Classical civilizations (Egypt, Greece, Rome)
- Non-European civilizations
- Rise and expansion of Europe
- Twentieth-century developments and transformations

United States History

- European exploration and colonization
- The American Revolution and the founding of the nation
- Growth and expansion of the Republic
- Twentieth-century developments and transformations

Political Science

- Nature and purpose of government
- Forms of government
- United States Constitution
- Rights and responsibilities of citizens
- State and local government

Anthropology, Sociology, and Psychology

- Anthropology
- Sociology
- Psychology

Economics

- The market
- Individuals and the market
- Economics' effect on population and resources
- Government's role in economics and economics' impact on government
- Economic systems
- Impact of technological developments on economy
- International economics

questions require you to combine several pieces of knowledge in order to formulate an integrated understanding. If you spend time on these questions, you will likely gain increased understanding and facility with the subject matter covered on the test. You may want to discuss these questions and your answers with a teacher or mentor.

Note that the questions marked with stars are open-ended, not multiple-choice. They are intended as *study* questions, not practice questions. Thinking about the answers to an open-ended question will improve your understanding of the fundamental concepts and will probably help you answer a number of related multiple-choice questions. For example, if you do what is suggested in this starred study topic:

> ★ Make your own "immigration timeline" of the nineteenth century, noting the decades during which immigrants from various countries or regions came to the United States in large numbers.

you have probably prepared yourself to answer the following multiple-choice question:

Immigration to the United States in the late nineteenth and early twentieth centuries differed from pre-Civil War immigration in that the groups that came later

(A) had a higher representation of people from southern and eastern Europe

(B) were generally wealthier and better educated

(C) assimilated faster and met with less prejudice

(D) were better able to escape the economic problems of some American cities

(The correct answer is (A).)

Geography

The world in spatial terms

Things to study

◆ Be able to read and interpret different kinds of maps and images (physical, topographical, political, and weather maps; aerial photographs and satellite images).

> ★ What is "map projection" and what kinds of decisions does it force mapmakers to make?

◆ Be familiar with longitude and latitude and their purposes.

◆ Be able to locate the equator and the International Dateline.

◆ Be able to use map legends to estimate distances, calculate scale, identify patterns represented in maps, and compute population density.

◆ Know the kinds of geographic features that make up the Earth (continents, oceans, seas, rivers, bays, mountain ranges, plateaus, valleys, plains, ice caps, tundra, forest, grassland, desert, island).

◆ Be able to locate on a map all seven continents, the four oceans, major seas and rivers, and major mountain ranges.

Places and regions

Things to study

▶ Be able to locate on a map major regions, countries, and cities of the world.

▶ Be familiar with the ways in which regions are categorized (e.g., political, physical, cultural).

> ★ What is the primary categorization of each of these regions, and why? Arab world, North Africa, Sub-Saharan Africa, Latin America, the Caribbean, North America, Western Europe, Eastern Europe, East Asia, South Central Asia, Southeast Asia, and Oceania

Physical systems

Things to study

Be able to answer definitional questions or questions that require making connections involving these systems and other social studies areas.

▶ The fundamental forces at work in cyclical systems like seasons, weather, and climate. (See more about these topics in the "Science" chapter.)

> ★ What is the difference between weather and climate?

▶ The basic mechanisms and consequences of physical changes that have short-term effects on Earth, including floods, droughts, and snowstorms.

▶ The basic mechanisms and consequences of physical changes that have long-term effects on Earth, including earthquakes (plate tectonics) and natural erosion.

> ★ How do earthquakes create mountain ranges?
>
> ★ What kinds of physical systems led to the creation of the Grand Canyon? What about Yosemite Valley?

Human systems

Things to study

Be able to answer definitional questions or questions that require making connections involving these phenomena and other social studies areas.

▶ Factors affecting settlement patterns — why some places are densely populated and others sparsely populated

▶ Major population trends in the United States in the nineteenth and twentieth centuries:

- Immigration patterns and their causes and effects

> ★ What kind of immigration patterns and effects were created by the Great Irish Famine?

- Parts of the country that grew faster than others in the twentieth century

- Trends in the ethnic composition of the United States population

- Functions of international organizations: the European Union, the World Trade Organization, the United Nations, NATO, the Organization of African Unity, OPEC

- Distinctions between developing and developed (industrialized) nations; the relative wealth of the largest nations

- Major trade relationships, especially those between the United States and other nations in the late twentieth and early twenty-first centuries

Environment and society

Things to study

Be able to answer definitional questions or questions that require making connections between these relationships and other social studies areas.

- The impact of the environment on human systems such as

  - Essentials like food, clothing, and shelter

  - Transportation and recreation

  - Economic and industrial systems

- Effects of human-initiated changes on the environment

  - Construction of houses, roads, and cities

  - Human-initiated fire

  - Water and air pollution

  - Waste disposal

★ What are the major effects on the environment and people when radioactive materials get into the environment either by leakage from storage or by an accident?

- Logging, deforestation, erosion, and desertification

- Global warming

- Ozone-layer depletion

- Natural resources — what they are and why they matter

  - Renewable and nonrenewable resources

  - Energy, mineral, food, and land resources

- Ecosystems and why understanding ecosystems is important

Uses of geography

Things to study

★ Think about how geography can be a helpful component when interpreting past or present events or phenomena such as

- The origins of the Industrial Revolution

- The current conflicts in the Middle East

- The political situations in Korea in the 1940's and 1950's and Vietnam in the 1960's and 1970's

- Decisions made by the United States government in the nineteenth century concerning Native Americans

---

World History

Prehistory and early civilizations

Things to study

Be able to recognize major characteristics of early civilizations, make connections and comparisons among them, and interpret visual or written selections relating to them.

▶ Major characteristics of human societies during the Paleolithic and Neolithic periods, with special concentration on hunter-gatherer societies and the agricultural revolution

▶ Development of settled societies, specialization, toolmaking, and the emergence of agriculture

▶ Major characteristics and contributions (architectural monuments, writing, technological capabilities) of the following ancient civilizations:

  • Mesopotamia (c. 3500–c. 2350 B.C.E.) (invention of writing, military expertise, city-states, Code of Hammurabi)

  • Indus River Valley (c. 2500–c. 1750 B.C.E.) (importance of water, city planning, agriculture)

  • Early China (c. 1500–c. 771 B.C.E.) (ancestor worship, manorialism)

  • Olmec society in Mesoamerica (c. 1200–c. 400 B.C.E.) (monumental sculpture, ceremonial centers, writing)

★ Find pictures of artifacts that survive from these civilizations so you can appreciate the beauty of what they made and accomplished. For each artifact you consider, think about what social, cultural, religious, and/or artistic values it reflects.

Classical civilizations (Egypt, Greece, Rome)

Things to study

Be able to recognize major characteristics and contributions of these civilizations, make connections and comparisons among them, and interpret visual or written selections relating to them.

▶ Ancient Egypt (c. 2700–c. 1090 B.C.E.)

  • Influence of geography on the civilization

  • Hieroglyphics and the Rosetta Stone

  • Religious rulership

  • Pyramids and the Valley of Kings

★ List as many ways as you can that the pyramids and burial customs of Egypt reflected aspects of Egyptian political, social, cultural, religious, bureaucratic (record keeping and writing), and artistic systems, elements, and values.

◆ Greece (c. 2000–c. 300 B.C.E.)

- Influence of geography on the civilization

- Mythology

- Social structure and the concepts of citizenship and democracy

> ★ How were the concepts of citizenship and democracy in ancient Greece similar and different from contemporary United States concepts of citizenship and democracy?

- Commerce, the city-state, and colonies

- Alexander the Great and the spread of Greek ideas

- Contrasting views of society: Athens and Sparta

> ★ How does a comparison of life in Athens and Sparta illuminate differences among nations in the world today?

- Important contributions (in drama, sculpture, sports, architecture, mathematics, and science) and the emphasis on human achievement

◆ Rome (c. 700 B.C.E.–500 C.E.)

- Influence of geography on the civilization

- Mythology

- Military domination, and its impact on the economy and society

> ★ How big did the Roman Empire get, with what borders, at its largest? In comparison, how small was it when it fell? What were the main reasons for the success at its largest point and its gradual shrinking?

- Government of Rome: republic to empire

- The establishment of "rule by law" and the concept of citizenship

- Origin and spread of Christianity, and Constantinople's role

- Important contributions in the areas of architecture, technology, science, literature, history, law, military science, and the importance of infrastructure (especially roads and aqueducts) to the empire

- Major causes for the decline and fall of the empire

Non-European civilizations

Things to study

Be able to recognize major characteristics of these civilizations, make connections and among them, and interpret visual or written selections relating to them.

◆ Islamic civilizations

- Origins, beliefs, and the spread of Islam

- Theological and cultural differences from other belief systems

> ★ What has been the role of Islam in African history?

- Present-day locations of largest populations of Islamic people

▶ India

• Caste system

★ Does the caste system survive in India today? How has the caste system shaped India's social, cultural, economic, and political histories?

• Hinduism (origins and beliefs)

• Muslim conquests

• Trade in spices, cloth, gems

▶ China

• Imperial government by trained bureaucracy

• Buddhism, Confucianism, Taoism

• Construction of the Great Wall

★ Why was the Great Wall built?

• Printing, compasses, gunpowder

• Significance and consequences of China's insularity

▶ Japan

• Feudalism

• Shintoism

• Buddhism

• Shoguns, emperors, samurai

★ What were the effects of Japan's isolation until the 1850's? How did Japan change after Admiral Perry's "opening" of Japan?

• Japan's relationship with China over the centuries

▶ Sub-Saharan Africa

• Trading empires

• Forest kingdoms

▶ Central and South America

• Mayans

• Aztecs

• Incas

• Exchange of food, diseases, and culture between Europeans and native Americans in Central and North America, and later, exchange of products and African slaves

★ Why were the Spanish able to defeat the Aztec and Incan empires?

Rise and expansion of Europe

Things to study

Be able to recognize major characteristics of these events, people, and trends; make connections and comparisons among them; and interpret visual or written selections relating to them.

▶ Economic, social, and political effects of feudalism

▶ The Black Death

▶ Early navigational advancements and discoveries, and their consequences and implications

• Voyages of Marco Polo, Magellan, Christopher Columbus, Vasco da Gama

▶ Renaissance

- New trade and economic practices that gave rise to the wealth of Italian city-states

- Contributions of Leonardo daVinci and Michelangelo in the arts and sciences

- Machiavelli's theory of government as expressed in *The Prince*

★ What does "Renaissance" mean? Why was the name given to this historical period?

★ What does the term "Renaissance man" or "Renaissance woman" mean, and how is the definition of the term (then and now) related to what happened during the Renaissance period?

▶ Reformation

- The theological and political issues that played a part in the Reformation

- The views and actions of Martin Luther and John Calvin and the consequences of these views and actions

▶ Scientific Revolution: scientific theories and discoveries by Newton, Copernicus, and Galileo

---

★ How did the Scientific Revolution change the way human perceived themselves and the universe and how did it change the methods of human inquiry?

▶ Enlightenment

- Major ideas that characterized Enlightenment thought; major contributions of Locke, Rousseau, and Jefferson

- How the political ideas of the Enlightenment affected the American and French Revolutions

▶ French Revolution and its impact

▶ Napoleon's goals, conquests, empire, and defeat

▶ Industrial Revolution

- How scientific and technological changes brought about massive social and cultural changes

- The factory system

- Inventions of Watt and Whitney and their effect on industrialization

▶ European imperialism

- European colonies in Asia and Africa at the end of the nineteenth century

- How Asia and Africa had been transformed by European commercial power

Twentieth-century developments and transformations

Things to study

Be able to recognize major characteristics of these events, people, and trends; make connections and comparisons among them; and interpret visual or written selections relating to them.

▶ Causes and consequences of the First World War

▶ Revolutions: Russian, Mexican, and Chinese Revolutions

▶ Worldwide economic depression in the 1930's and the political, social, and economic impact

▶ Rise of communism in the Soviet Union and fascism in Germany, Italy, and Japan

- Causes and consequences of the Second World War; the Holocaust

- Economic and military power shifts since 1945, including reasons for the rise of Germany and Japan

- Origin and meaning of the Cold War; collapse of the Soviet Union

- Post-Second World War decolonization in Africa and Asia and increased democracy in Europe, including

  - India and Pakistan in 1947

  - Sub-Saharan nations in 1960

  - Kenya, Angola, and Mozambique in the 1960's and 1970's

  - Nations in Eastern Europe, the Balkans, and the former Soviet Union in the 1980's and 1990's

- Rise of a global culture

> ★ What are the main reasons that a global culture emerged in the twentieth century? What are the consequences of this global culture?

- Rise of a global economy

- Major scientific advances: atomic power, atomic bomb, space travel, satellite technology, computers, genetic manipulation, Internet, e-commerce

United States History

> ★ Make your own timeline of United States history, with the centuries beginning with 1400, 1500, 1600, and so on (recognizing, of course, that Native Americans were here for thousands of years before that). Put each of the events listed below on your timeline in the correct century, then describe important trends in political, diplomatic, social, religious, artistic, and economic history.

European exploration and colonization

Things to study

Be able to recognize characteristics of these events, people, and trends; make connections and comparisons among them; and interpret visual or written selections relating to them.

- The numerous unique and well-developed Native American cultures in North America, most prominently the Inuits (Eskimos), Anasazi (cliff dwellers), Northwest Indians (Kwakiutl), Plains Indians, the Mound Builders, Iroquois

- Causes, purposes, and results of exploration and colonization of North America by Spain, France, and England

- Interactions between the Native Americans and the Europeans

- Colonial culture, society, religion, economy, and political institutions from the perspective of various inhabitants: large landowners, farmers, artisans, women, slaves, and colonial leaders

The American Revolution and the founding of the nation

Things to study

Be able to recognize characteristics of these events, people, and trends; make connections and comparisons among them; and interpret visual or written selections relating to them.

▶ Causes of the American Revolution

▶ Major ideas in the Declaration of Independence and their impact

▶ Major ideas in the Articles of Confederation

> ★ What were the weaknesses in the Articles of Confederation that eventually led to its replacement by the Constitution? Why were the Articles written in this way in the first place?

▶ Key individuals and their roles and major beliefs: King George, John Adams, George Washington, Thomas Jefferson, Benjamin Franklin, Thomas Paine

▶ The Constitution, how and when it came into being, including major compromises, and the addition of the Bill of Rights

> ★ Name some ways the Constitution affects our lives today.

▶ The origin of political parties in the United States

> ★ What was the *Marbury* v. *Madison* decision in the Supreme Court and what did it establish?

Growth and expansion of the republic

Things to study

Be able to recognize characteristics of these events, people, and trends; make connections and comparisons among them; and interpret visual or written selections relating to them.

▶ Origins of slavery in the United States, how it is addressed in the United States Constitution, and slavery's effects on political, social, religious, economic, and cultural developments among African Americans and in American society generally

▶ Westward expansion: Louisiana Purchase, Lewis and Clark expedition, and the acquisition of Florida, Texas, Oregon, and California

> ★ What was "Manifest Destiny" and how did it influence the expansion of United States territory?

▶ Relationships with Mexico (Mexican War and Cession), Canada (War of 1812), and Europe (Monroe Doctrine)

▶ The story of the "Trail of Tears," including the Removal Act (broken treaties, massacres, conflicts, and displacement of Native Americans)

▶ Impact of technological and agricultural innovations before the Civil War — Whitney's cotton gin, McCormick's reaper, Fulton's steamboat, and the steam locomotive

▶ Reasons for and consequences of waves of immigration from Europe in the nineteenth century

★ Make your own "immigration timeline" of the nineteenth century, noting the decades during which immigrants from various countries or regions came to the United States in large numbers.

◗ Civil War and Reconstruction

- The economic and cultural differences between North and South

- The abolitionist movement

- The women's movement

- The Fugitive Slave Act and the Dred Scott case

- Key roles and actions of Abraham Lincoln, Jefferson Davis, Frederick Douglass, William Lloyd Garrison, Harriet Tubman, Harriet Beecher Stowe, and John Brown

- Key events leading to declaration of secession and war

- Major points in the Gettysburg Address, Emancipation Proclamation, and the basic provisions and impact of the 13th, 14th, and 15th Amendments to the United States Constitution

- Impact of Reconstruction policies on the South then and now

- Segregation after the Civil War, including the Supreme Court decision in *Plessy* v. *Ferguson*

◗ Business and labor after the Civil War

- Bankers and entrepreneurs Andrew Carnegie, John D. Rockefeller, and J. P. Morgan: their industries and the changes in American business that they represented

- Urban conditions (living conditions, child labor, social stratification)

- Waves of immigrants after the Civil War

★ Post-Civil War immigration can be viewed in terms of the "melting pot" analogy or in terms of "pluralism" or "multiculturalism." What does this distinction mean, and why is it important?

- The progressive movement's responses to the problems of industrial society (e.g., church and humanitarian groups' actions)

- The rise of the labor movement

◗ America's imperialism at the turn of the century as evidenced in the Spanish-American War, the building of the Panama Canal, and Theodore Roosevelt's "Big Stick Diplomacy"

◗ Women's rights movement and its leaders

Twentieth-century developments and transformations

Things to study

Be able to recognize characteristics of these events, people, and trends; make connections and comparisons among them; and interpret visual or written selections relating to them.

◗ America's role in the First World War and postwar isolationism

◗ Important developments in the 1920's

- The Harlem Renaissance (Zora Neale Hurston, Langston Hughes)

- Prohibition

- The rise of mass-production techniques and new technologies with far-reaching effects (e.g., the automobile and electricity)

▶ Women's suffrage (the movement and the amendment)

▶ The Great Depression and the New Deal — causes of the Depression; impact on various groups in the United States; Franklin D. Roosevelt and the New Deal (Works Progress Administration; Social Security; National Labor Relations Board)

▶ America's role in the Second World War and consequences at home and abroad

- Internment of Japanese Americans

- Decision to drop atomic bombs on Hiroshima and Nagasaki and the consequences

- Postwar consequences (e.g., the baby boom)

▶ American society in the second half of the twentieth century

- America's role in the Cold War

- Korean War — major causes and outcomes

- McCarthyism

- Desegregation in schools

> ★ What was the Supreme Court's decision in *Brown* v. *Board of Education of Topeka*? How was the later decision in *University of California* v. *Bakke* related to another important educational issue in the twentieth century?

- Vietnam War — major causes and outcomes

- Civil rights movement, women's movement, peace movement

- Environmentalism

- Rise of the consumer society

- Changing demographics — ethnic and cultural identities and associations and how they are expressed and play a role in society

- Development of computers and information systems and the impact on the economy and jobs

Political Science

Nature and purpose of government

Things to study

Descriptions or excerpts will be given, accompanied by questions asking about these issues.

▶ Definition of "government"

▶ Purposes of government (conflict resolution, collective decision-making, etc.)

▶ Intended and unintended consequences of the ideals and philosophies of various forms of government (e.g., in terms of social welfare and human rights)

> ★ Compare the intended and unintended consequences of feudalism, communism, monarchy, and liberal democracies in some well-known cases: in trying to solve some problems, what problems did the founders create?

Forms of government

Things to study

Be able to identify major characteristics of these forms of government and differentiate among them.

- Parliamentary systems
- Federalism
- Constitutional structures
- Unitary structures

> ★ Compare the major features of a democratic government with those of other forms of government.
>
> ★ Why were the *Magna Carta*, Mayflower Compact, and the Declaration of Independence such milestone documents in the political history of the world?

United States Constitution

Things to study

Questions involving excerpts from the Declaration of Independence or Constitution or questions about major ideas in these documents may be asked, in addition to specific roles and responsibilities in the federal government.

- The major values, beliefs, principles expressed in the Declaration of Independence, Constitution, and the Bill of Rights
- The "separation of powers" among the three branches of the federal government and the major responsibilities of each branch

> ★ How does the electoral college work?
>
> ★ What is the line of authority if the President and vice president are incapacitated? Who are the next few in line?

Rights and responsibilities of citizens

Things to study

Descriptions or excerpts will be given, accompanied by questions asking about these topics.

- The meaning and importance of the following rights of democratic citizens: freedom of speech, religion, press, assembly, petition, and privacy
- The importance of the following economic rights: property rights, the right to choose one's work, the right to join or not join a labor union, and the right to apply for copyrights and patents
- Balancing citizens' rights with the common good
- Citizens' legal obligations (to obey the law, serve as juror, and pay taxes) and civic-minded obligations (becoming informed about issues and candidates, voting, volunteering, and serving in the military or alternative service)
- Understand the naturalization process by which immigrants become citizens of the United States (literacy, language, and other requirements)

State and local government

Things to study

Questions comparing various levels of government and their responsibilities will be asked.

▶ Major responsibilities of state governments

▶ Relationship between state governments and the federal government

▶ Major responsibilities of local governments

▶ Basic principles of tribal sovereignty

Anthropology, Sociology, and Psychology

Anthropology

Things to study

Questions about major goals and methods may be asked. Visual or written selections may be given, accompanied by questions about anthropological interpretations.

▶ Basic goals of anthropology and archaeology

▶ The two branches of anthropology: physical and cultural

▶ How kinship (family) patterns address basic human needs and concerns and how they interact with social institutions

▶ Social institutions (political structures, faith communities, clubs, ethnic communities, sports organizations) and their visible outgrowths (customs, symbols, celebrations)

▶ Social stratification of individuals, groups, and institutions (status, social class, social mobility, class conflict)

▶ Human experience and cultural expression (language, stories, music, dance, artifacts, traditions, beliefs, spirituality, values, behavior) and how they contribute to the development and transmission of culture

Sociology

Things to study

Questions about major goals and methods may be asked. Visual or written selections may be given, accompanied by questions about sociological interpretations.

▶ Basic concepts in sociology — networks; primary and secondary groups; social solidarity and conflict; role; status; norms; minority; ethnicity; group; institution

▶ Socialization and acculturation — understand the role of socialization in society and the roles of positive and negative sanctions in the socialization process

▶ Social stratification and social mobility

▶ Ethnic groups and societal change — understand the study of populations, including the impact on society of population growth, distribution, migration, and immigration

▶ Stereotypes, biases, values, ideals — understand the concepts of ethnocentrism, cultural relativity, prejudice, discrimination, stereotyping, pluralism, multicultural diversity

Psychology

Things to study

Questions about major goals and methods may be asked. Visual or written selections may be given, accompanied by questions about psychological interpretations.

▶ Basic concepts and approaches

- Cognitive development
- Behavioralism
- Physiological influences
- Social influences
- Emotions
- Personality
- Self-concept
- Learning
- Individual
- Needs and wants
- Differences
- Motives
- Perception
- Values
- Character

▶ Human development and growth — four stages (infancy, childhood, adolescence, adulthood)

▶ Human behavior — how beliefs, experiences, attitudes, conditioning, consequences, heredity, and other factors affect an individual's behavior

▶ Gender roles and differences — varying influences (e.g., physiological, social, cognitive, etc.)

Economics

The market

Things to study

Questions about major concepts and definitions may be asked. Visual or written selections may be given, accompanied by questions about these concepts.

▶ Scarcity

▶ Needs and wants

▶ Resources

▶ Cost

▶ Opportunity cost

▶ Property

▶ Capital

▶ Goods

▶ Markets

▶ Price

▶ Competition

▶ Supply and demand

▶ Production and consumption

▶ Inflation, deflation, recession, depression

▶ Trade and barter

★ Why is it claimed that the concept of "scarcity" is the basis for the discipline of economics?

- Know the basic roles of the following institutions:

  - Corporations

  - Labor unions

  - Banks

  - Nonprofit institutions

  - Credit companies

  - Insurance companies

  - Stock markets

- Private versus public goods

- Private versus public services

Individuals and the market

Things to study

Questions about major concepts and definitions may be asked. Visual or written selections may be given, accompanied by questions about these concepts.

- Employment and unemployment: official United States government definitions of employment, unemployment, and "labor force"

- Labor

  - Minimum wage

  - Cost-of-living raise

  - Current types of skills that workers need

  - Effects of rapid technological change and international competition on labor in general and individuals

- Distribution of wealth

  - Be able to interpret tables and graphs having to do with distribution of wealth.

★ What are some of the government mechanisms that have been used in the United States for redistributing wealth? What are the dangers of too much government redistribution versus the dangers of too much wealth concentrated in a small percentage of the population?

- Marketing: why companies invest in marketing, customer service, advertising, credit

Economics' effect on population and resources

Things to study

Questions about major concepts and definitions may be asked. Visual or written selections may be given, accompanied by questions about these concepts.

- Private ownership, private enterprise, profits

- Division of labor and specialization

- Natural, capital, and human resources

Government's role in economics and economics' impact on government

Things to study

Questions about major concepts and definitions may be asked. Visual or written selections may be given, accompanied by questions about these concepts.

- Reasons governments levy taxes
- Government's role in maintaining the country's currency
- National debt
- Federal Reserve System
- Consumer Price Index
- Federal government's budget ("balanced," "deficit," "surplus")
- Gross National Product

Economic systems

Things to study

Questions about major concepts and definitions may be asked. Visual or written selections may be given, accompanied by questions about these concepts.

Major characteristics of

- Traditional economies
- Command economies
- Free-market economies
- Communism
- Socialism
- Capitalism

Impact of technological developments on economy

Things to study

★ What has been the impact of satellite systems (wireless technology), the Internet, and robotics (in assembly lines and warehouses) on the United States and world economies? How is e-commerce changing the United States and world economies?

International economics

Things to study

▶ Basic definitions of

- Imports and exports
- Tariffs and quotas
- Economic sanctions

▶ Arguments for and against "free trade"

▶ Currencies and exchange rates: the effects when the dollar gains or loses value relative to other currencies

Chapter 6
Science: Study Topics

▶ ▶ ▶ ▶ ▶ ▶ ▶ ▶ ▶ ▶ ▶ ▶

Science: Study Topics

The "Science" component of the *Elementary Education: Content Knowledge* test covers Earth science, life science, physical science, science as inquiry, science in personal and social perspectives, history and nature of science, and unifying processes.

The "Science" section of the test was designed to align with Standard 2c of the *Program Standards for Elementary Teacher Preparation* published by NCATE (National Council for Accreditation of Teacher Education):

> Candidates know, understand, and use fundamental concepts in the subject matter of science — including physical, life, and Earth and space sciences — as well as concepts in science and technology, science in personal and social perspectives, the history and nature of science, the unifying concepts of science, and the inquiry processes scientists use in discovery of new knowledge to build a base for scientific and technological literacy.

The "Science" component of the test focuses on fundamental scientific concepts, principles, and interrelationships within the context of real-world, meaningful scientific phenomena, problems, and issues. Basic understanding of the Earth, life processes, and physical matter and energy is crucial, as is an understanding of the nature of science as a complex human enterprise with a distinct philosophy and methodology and a place and role in society.

Using the topic lists that follow: You are not expected to be an expert on the topics that follow. But you should understand the major characteristics or aspects of each topic and be able to relate the topic to various situations presented in the test questions, e.g., a map, picture, graph, quotation, etc. For instance, here is one of the topic lists in "Earth Science," under "Earth and universe":

- Stars and galaxies

- The solar system and planets

- Earth, Sun, and Moon relationships (orbits, rotations, tilt, cycles)

- Motion of the heavens

Using textbooks, state standards documents, and other sources as needed, make sure you review basic materials on all of these topics. On the test you may be asked direct questions on one or more of these topics, or you may be asked to choose a correct interpretation of a situation that is described (e.g., a description of the shape and positions of the Moon on a certain night).

Special questions marked with stars: Interspersed throughout the topic lists are questions that are preceded by stars (★) and outlined in boxes. These questions are intended to test your knowledge of fundamental concepts in the topic area. Some of these questions are derived from typical questions children ask, and answering them usually requires a significant amount of content knowledge. Other questions require you to combine several pieces of knowledge in

Here is an overview of the areas within "Science":

Earth Science ————————————

> Structure of the Earth system
> Process of the Earth system
> Earth history
> Earth and universe

Life Science ————————————

> Structure and function of living systems
> Reproduction and heredity
> Regulation and behavior
> Biological evolution
> Interdependence of organisms

Physical Science ————————————

> Structure and properties of matter
> Forces and motions
> Energy
> Interactions of energy and matter

Science as Inquiry ————————————

> Inquiry process
> Understandings about scientific inquiry

Science in Personal and ————————
Social Perspectives

> Personal health
> Science, technology, and society

History and Nature of Science ————————

> Science as a human endeavor
> Historical perspectives in science
> Science as a career

Unifying Processes

[No sub-areas]

---

order to formulate an integrated understanding. If you spend time on these questions, you will likely gain increased understanding and facility with the subject matter covered on the test. You may want to discuss these questions and your answers with a teacher or mentor.

Note that these questions marked with stars are open-ended, not multiple-choice. They are intended as *study* questions, not practice questions. Thinking about the answers to these open-ended

questions will improve your understanding of fundamental concepts and will probably help you answer a number of related multiple-choice questions. For example, if you answer and understand the concept behind this starred study topic:

> ★ Why do we see our breath on a cold day but not on a warm day?

you will probably have prepared yourself to answer the following multiple-choice question:

> Which of the following best explains why moisture condenses on the inside of a glass windowpane in a room being warmed by an electric heater shortly after a cold front moves into the area?
>
> (A) The electric heater releases moisture into the air.
>
> (B) Water molecules in the room air are attracted to the glass.
>
> (C) The cold front brings with it large amounts of moisture.
>
> (D) The room air near the window is cooled, lowering its capacity for water vapor.

(The answer is (D), since the cooler air, like that closest to the window, cannot hold as much water vapor as the warm air in the rest of the room, so the water condenses and appears as water droplets on the windowpane. In the same way, the cool air of winter cannot hold as much water vapor from the moisture of our breath as the warm air of summer.)

Earth Science

Structure of the Earth system

Things to study

Descriptions, visuals, or other examples will be presented, accompanied by questions relating to one or more of these topics. You may also be asked definitional questions about these topics.

◆ Structure and properties of solid Earth

- The major layers of Earth

> ★ What is the "inside" of Earth like?

- Plate tectonics
- The three major types of rocks that make up Earth and how they are formed
- How soil is formed
- Minerals

> ★ What is the difference between a rock and a mineral?
>
> ★ What substances are found in concrete?
>
> ★ What are fossils and how are they formed?

◆ Structure and properties of the hydrosphere (oceans)

- The difference between saltwater and freshwater bodies of water and the kinds of minerals contained in salt water
- The four major oceans
- The physical features at the shore
- The physical features beneath the surface of the oceans

◆ Structure and properties of the atmosphere

- The various gases that comprise the atmosphere
- How the atmosphere is structured in layers

> ★ In which layer of the atmosphere is the aurora borealis displayed? What is the cause of this natural light show?
>
> ★ What is air pressure and how is it measured?

Process of the Earth system

Things to study

Descriptions, visuals, or other examples will be presented, accompanied by questions relating to one or more of these topics. You may also be asked definitional questions about these topics.

◗ Processes of the solid Earth

• Weathering

> ★ Why do monuments in Egypt last for thousands of years, while the same monuments transported to northern climates deteriorate very quickly?

• Erosion
• Volcanoes

> ★ What is the "Ring of Fire"?
>
> ★ What causes a volcano to erupt?

• Earthquakes

> ★ What causes earthquakes?

◗ Processes of the hydrosphere (oceans)

• Currents
• Waves
• Tides

> ★ What causes tides? What do "low tide" and "high tide" mean?
>
> ★ The greatest difference in water level between a low tide and a high tide occurs because of what alignment of the Moon, Sun, and Earth?

◗ Processes of the atmosphere

• The "water cycle"

• What clouds are made of and how they form and change

• The major types of clouds

• Different types of precipitation

• Climate and weather:
— Wind belts and pressure zones
— Interaction of air masses and fronts

> ★ How do storms form?

— Changes in weather from season to season

> ★ How do oceans affect climate?
>
> ★ Why do we see our breath on a cold day but not on a warm day?

— Weather maps: isobar and isotherm

Earth history

Things to study

Questions drawing on your understanding of the major elements of these topics will be asked.

◗ Origin of the Earth

◗ Paleontology

◗ The rock record

◗ Geologic time scale

Earth and universe

Things to study

Descriptions, visuals, or other examples will be presented, accompanied by questions relating to one or more of these topics. You may also be asked definitional questions about these topics.

▶ Stars and galaxies

▶ The solar system and planets

> ★ Why do the planets circle the Sun?
>
> ★ How does a solar eclipse occur?
>
> ★ How are the inner planets of the solar system different from the outer planets?

▶ Earth, Sun, and Moon relationships (orbits, rotations, tilt, cycles)

> ★ What causes the seasons on Earth? What is the positional relationship of the Sun and Earth at each season?

▶ Motion of the heavens

> ★ Why do the stars appear to move across the sky each night, although the pattern of stars stays the same?
>
> ★ Why are different stars seen in different seasons?
>
> ★ Why does the position of a planet as seen from Earth change in relation to the background of stars?
>
> ★ Why do stars twinkle while planets do not?

▶ Comets and meteors

Life Science

Structure and function of living systems

Things to study

Questions drawing on your understanding of the major elements of these topics will be asked.

▶ Cells: basic structure and function

> ★ Are most cells flat? What do electron-microscope pictures show us about cell shape?

▶ Cell processes

  • Photosynthesis

> ★ What makes a plant bend toward the light? What is the scientific term associated with this?
>
> ★ Why are roots, stems, and leaves important to plants?

  • Diffusion
  • Osmosis
  • Active transport
  • Transpiration
  • Respiration

▶ Human organs and organ systems

> ★ How does the human circulatory system work?
>
> ★ How does the human digestive system work?

Reproduction and heredity

Things to study

Questions drawing on your understanding of the major elements of these topics will be asked.

◗ Sexual/asexual mechanics of reproduction

◗ Growth and development

◗ Patterns of inheritance of traits (genetics)

> ★ What are dominant and recessive traits?
>
> ★ How can both of my parents have brown eyes and I have blue eyes?

◗ Molecular basis of heredity (DNA, genes, chromosomes)

Regulation and behavior

Things to study

Questions drawing on your understanding of the major elements of these topics will be asked.

◗ Life cycle

◗ Responses to external stimuli

◗ Controlling the internal environment

◗ Instinctual behaviors such as migration, hibernation, living in societies

◗ Conditioned behavior

Biological evolution

Things to study

Questions drawing on your understanding of the major elements of these topics will be asked.

◗ Unity and diversity of life

◗ Adaptation

◗ Natural selection

> ★ What is meant by "survival of the fittest"?

◗ Extinction

> ★ Will humans always be present on Earth?

Interdependence of organisms

Things to study

Questions drawing on your understanding of the major elements of these topics will be asked.

◗ Populations

◗ Communities

◗ Ecosystems

• Food chain

> ★ What happens if certain kinds of organisms, such as edible plants, are introduced or removed from a food chain?

• Food web

> ★ How do food chains become food webs?

◗ Growth and regulation of populations

Physical Science

Structure and properties of matter

Things to study

Descriptions, visuals, or other examples will be presented, accompanied by questions relating to one or more of these topics. You may also be asked definitional questions about these topics.

▶ Physical properties of matter

> ★ Does air take up space?

▶ Conservation of matter

▶ Physical and chemical changes of matter

> ★ Sometimes when two chemicals are combined, a chemical reaction takes place. What are some of the signs of such a chemical reaction?

▶ Mixtures and solution

▶ Atoms and elements

> ★ What is the periodic table and what information does it contain?

▶ Molecules and compounds
- Chemical notation for molecules (e.g., CO_2)
- Simple chemical equations (C + O = CO)

Forces and motions

Things to study

Descriptions, visuals, or other examples will be presented, accompanied by questions relating to one or more of these topics. You may also be asked definitional questions about these topics.

▶ Types of motion
- Speed, distance, and time relationships
- Acceleration

> ★ Are the hands of a clock accelerating?

- Circular motion
- Relative motion

> ★ When you are driving side by side with another car, why does the other car appear to be not moving, even though it is moving with the same speed as your car?

▶ Forces and laws of motion
- Newton's laws of motion

> ★ What causes an object in motion to accelerate or slow down?

- Friction
- Centripetal force
- Newton's law of gravitation

> ★ What is the difference between weight and mass?

- Equilibrium

> ★ Describe various ways in which an object can have several forces acting on it and still be at rest.

Energy

Things to study

Descriptions, visuals, or other examples will be presented, accompanied by questions relating to one or more of these topics. You may also be asked definitional questions about these topics.

◗ Forms of energy

> ★ How is the energy of a rock sitting on the top of a hill different from the energy of a rock sitting at the bottom of the same hill?

◗ Transfer and conservation of energy

> ★ Why does rubbing your hands together make them warmer?
>
> ★ How does the energy associated with a bicycle change as it speeds up going downhill?

◗ Simple machines

Interactions of energy and matter

Things to study

Descriptions, visuals, or other examples will be presented, accompanied by questions relating to one or more of these topics. You may also be asked definitional questions about these topics.

◗ Wave phenomena (waves in water; sound waves; earthquake waves)

◗ Electromagnetic spectrum

  • Light waves

  • Nonvisible waves
    — Infrared waves
    — Radio waves
    — Microwaves
    — X-rays
    — Gamma rays

> ★ How do electromagnetic waves differ from sound waves and water waves? What is an example of how each of the nonvisible waves is used in day-to-day life?

◗ Light and color

> ★ Why do we see an apple as being red?

◗ Mirrors and lenses

> ★ Why does a mirror reflect light while a lens lets it pass through?
>
> ★ Which types of lenses magnify and which types produce an image reduced in size?
>
> ★ How do lenses help nearsighted and farsighted people?

◗ Heat and temperature

  • Heat by conduction, convection, and radiation

◗ Electricity and magnetism

> ★ How does an electrical circuit work?
>
> ★ How does a compass work?

- Ways that electrical energy can be converted to heat, light, and motion

> ★ Name some appliances that can convert electrical energy to each of the following: heat energy, light energy, and energy of motion.

◗ Sound

> ★ Why do we hear the sound that accompanies a lightning strike later than we see the flash of light?
>
> ★ What are echoes and what causes them?

Science as Inquiry

Inquiry process

Things to study

Examples of situations will be given, accompanied by questions asking about the most appropriate strategies and decisions.

◗ Using appropriate questioning techniques; developing testable questions and hypotheses

◗ Planning and conducting simple investigations; using controlled and experimental variables

> ★ How are control variables and experimental variables used in scientific investigations?

◗ Gathering data with the tools of science; choosing the appropriate tools

◗ Organizing and using data to construct reasonable explanations; displaying data; analyzing data

◗ Communicating investigations and explanations

Understandings about scientific inquiry

Things to study

> ★ How do different questions require different approaches and tools in the investigation stage?
>
> ★ How do mathematics and technology assist in different kinds of scientific inquiry?
>
> ★ What are some examples of measuring instruments?
>
> ★ How does "skepticism" relate to scientific inquiry?
>
> ★ How do ethics relate to scientific inquiry?
>
> ★ What ways other than the inquiry process have led to important new scientific ideas or discoveries?

Science in Personal and Social Perspectives

Personal health

Things to study

Descriptions, visuals, or other examples will be presented, accompanied by questions relating to one or more of these topics. You may also be asked definitional questions about these topics.

- Nutrition
- Exercise and fitness

> ★ How does physical fitness help a person?

- Safety and well-being
- Communicable diseases

> ★ In what ways can infection spread?

- Substance abuse

> ★ How do drugs, alcohol, and tobacco affect the body?
>
> ★ How are prescription medicines and over-the-counter medicines different?

- Common diseases (cold, flu, measles, chicken pox), viral and bacterial causes, how vaccinations work

Science, technology, and society

Things to study

Examples of situations will be given, accompanied by questions asking about the most appropriate strategies and decisions.

- Technological design
  - Identifying the need for a tool
  - Proposing various designs and considering constraints and alternatives
  - Implementing the design
  - Evaluating the impact

- Science's links with technology
  - Science driving the need for new technology
  - Technology providing essential instruments for science
  - Both science and technology involving risk, choices, and constraints

- Acid rain, greenhouse effect, and other ways that human activity affects the environment in adverse ways

- The "Science-Technology-Society" (S-T-S) method

> ★ What can a community do about air pollution or water pollution?
>
> ★ What should a worker do if he or she finds that food is being handled in unsafe ways in the workplace?
>
> ★ Is lead in drinking water dangerous? If so, what should a family do?

History and Nature of Science

Science as a human endeavor

Things to study

Descriptions or situations will be given, accompanied by questions asking about the human aspects of the endeavor.

> ★ What kinds of human abilities does science require?
>
> ★ What is an example of a complex scientific endeavor involving hundreds of people working on a major scientific endeavor? What is an example of a single scientist working on a relatively straightforward question?

Historical perspectives in science

Things to study

Descriptions or situations will be given, accompanied by questions asking about the historical perspective of the endeavor.

> ★ Why was acceptance of some major scientific explanations so difficult (e.g., those of Copernicus, Galileo, Darwin)?
>
> ★ How has most scientific work been built on earlier knowledge over the centuries? How is this different from the rare, major advances that break with predecessors and have long-lasting effects?

Science as a career

Things to study

Descriptions or situations will be given, accompanied by questions asking about issues related to scientists' work.

- Science careers in colleges, universities, industry, research institutes, government agencies
- Day-to-day work of a scientist: in the field, in the laboratory, in the classroom, at the computer

> ★ What are the shared values of professional scientists? What is an example of an ethical code that scientists are expected to adhere to?
>
> ★ Why is communication an essential part of being a scientist?

Unifying Processes

Things to study

There are a number of conceptual schemes and procedural schemes that are used across all science disciplines. These underlying principles are embodied in different ways in different disciplines (e.g., earth science, botany, medical research), but they transcend disciplinary boundaries and provide students with powerful ideas to help them understand the natural world.

- Systems, order, and organization
- Evidence, models, and explanation
- Change, constancy, and measurement
- Evolution and equilibrium
- Form and function

> ★ Why is each of these ideas considered a crucial conceptual scheme or procedural scheme and how does each one cut across the scientific disciplines?

Chapter 7

Don't Be Defeated by
Multiple-Choice Questions

▶   ▶   ▶   ▶   ▶   ▶   ▶   ▶   ▶   ▶   ▶   ▶

Why the Multiple-Choice Tests Take Time

When you take the practice questions, you will see that there are very few simple identification questions of the "Which of the following authors wrote *Moby Dick*?" sort. When The Praxis Series Assessments were first being developed by teachers and teacher educators across the country, it was almost universally agreed that prospective teachers should be able to analyze situations, synthesize material, and apply knowledge to specific examples. In short, they should be able to think as well as to recall specific facts, figures, or formulas. Consequently, you will find that you are being asked to think and to solve problems on your test. Such activity takes more time than simply answering identification questions.

In addition, questions that require you to analyze situations, synthesize material, and apply knowledge are usually longer than are simple identification questions. The Praxis Series test questions often present you with something to read (a case study, a sample of student work, a chart or graph) and ask you questions based on your reading. Strong reading skills are required, and you must read carefully. Both on this test and as a teacher, you will need to process and use what you read efficiently.

If you know your reading skills are not strong, you may want to take a reading course. College campuses have reading labs that can help you strengthen your reading skills.

Understanding Multiple-Choice Questions

You will probably notice that the word order in multiple-choice questions (or syntax) is different from the word order you're used to seeing in ordinary things you read, like newspapers or textbooks. One of the reasons for this difference is that many such questions contain the phrase "which of the following."

The purpose of the phrase "which of the following" is to limit your choice of answers only to the list given. For example, look at this question.

Which of the following is a flavor made from beans?

(A) Strawberry

(B) Cherry

(C) Vanilla

(D) Mint

You may know that chocolate and coffee are flavors made from beans also. But they are not listed, and the question asks you to select from among the list that follows ("which of the following"). So the answer has to be the only bean-derived flavor in the list: vanilla.

Notice that the answer can be submitted for the phrase "which of the following." In the question above, you could insert "vanilla" for "which of the following" and have the sentence "Vanilla is a flavor made from beans." Sometimes it helps to cross out "which of the following" and insert the various choices. You may want to give this technique a try as you answer various multiple-choice questions in the practice test.

Also, looking carefully at the "which of the following" phrase helps you to focus on what the question is asking you to find and on the answer choices. In the simple example above, all of the answer choices are flavors. Your job is to decide which of the flavors is the one made from beans.

The vanilla bean question is pretty straightforward. But the phrase "which of the following" can also be found in more challenging questions. Look at this question.

> Entries in outlines are generally arranged according to which of the following relationships of ideas?
>
> (A) Literal and inferential
>
> (B) Concrete and abstract
>
> (C) Linear and recursive
>
> (D) Main and subordinate

The placement of "which of the following" tells you that the list of choices is a list of "relationships of ideas." What are you supposed to find as an answer? You are supposed to find the choice that describes how entries, or ideas, in outlines are related.

Sometimes it helps to put the question in your own words. Here, you could paraphrase the question as "How are outlines usually organized?" Since the ideas in outlines usually appear as main ideas and subordinate ideas, the answer is (D).

TIP Don't be put off by words you don't understand. It might be easy to be upset by words like "recursive" or "inferential". Read carefully to understand the question and look for an answer that fits. An outline is something you are probably familiar with and expect to teach to your students. So slow down, and use what you know. Don't make the questions more difficult than they are.

Don't read for "hidden meanings" or "tricks." There are no "trick questions" on The Praxis Series Subject Assessments. They are intended to be serious, straightforward tests of subject knowledge.

You may find that it helps you to circle or underline each of the critical details of the question in your test book so that you don't miss any of them. It's only by looking at all parts of the question carefully that you will have all of the information you need to answer the question.

Circle or underline the critical parts of what is being asked in this question.

> According to research, which of the following is the single most <u>important home-based activity</u> for <u>preschool children</u> in <u>building</u> the <u>knowledge</u> required for children's eventual <u>success in reading</u>?
>
> (A) Children's memorizing nursery rhymes
>
> (B) Families' talking about school
>
> (C) Parents' reading aloud to children ‧
>
> (D) Parents' teaching the alphabet

Here is one possible way you may have annotated the question:

> According to research, which of the following is the single most important home-based activity for <u>preschool children</u> in building the knowledge required for children's eventual <u>success in reading</u>?
>
> (A) Children's memorizing nursery rhymes
>
> (B) Families' talking about school
>
> (C) Parents' reading aloud to children
>
> (D) Parents' teaching the alphabet

After spending a minute with the question, you can probably see that you are being asked to find the activity for preschoolers that will be most helpful for future reading skills. (The answer is (C).) The important thing is figuring out what the question is asking. Figuring out the answer is the second step. With enough practice, you should be able to figure out what any question is asking. Knowing the answer is, of course, a different matter, but you have to understand a question before you can answer it.

It takes more work to understand "which of the following" questions when there are even more words in a question. Questions that require application or interpretation invariably require more reading than straight naming-the-activity questions would.

Consider this question.

> "While we abhor communist domination of Eastern Europe, we must realize that it would be impractical to try to free captured peoples. Rather we must use our power to prevent further expansion of the Red Menace."

> The analysis above of the situation in Europe after the Second World War provided the rationale for which of the following United States policies?

> (A) Flexible response

> (B) Massive retaliation

> (C) Liberation

> (D) Containment

Given the placement of the phrase "which of the following," you can tell that the list of answer choices is a list of "policies." You are supposed to pick the policy that is defended in the analysis given.

Being able to select the right answer depends on your understanding of the analysis given. Try to rephrase the selection in your own words. You might come up with something like "We cannot free the people of Eastern Europe who are dominated by communism, but we can use our power to prevent further domination by communists." This helps lead you to the correct answer, (D). "Containment" is the name given to the policy of trying to "contain" the spread of communism.

Understanding Questions Containing "NOT," "LEAST," "EXCEPT"

In addition to "which of the following" and details that must be understood, the words "NOT," "EXCEPT," and "LEAST" often make comprehension of test questions more difficult. These words are always capitalized when they appear in The Praxis Series test questions, but they are easily (and frequently) overlooked.

For the following test question, determine what kind of answer you're looking for and what the details of the question are.

> Which of the following is NOT a way in which mammals keep themselves warm in winter?

> (A) Shivering

> (B) Perspiring

> (C) Fluffing out coat hair

> (D) Contracting certain blood vessels

You're looking for the way that is NOT used by mammals. (B) is the answer — that is, all of the other choices *are* ways in which mammals keep themselves warm.

TIP It's easy to get confused while you're processing the information to answer a question with a LEAST, NOT, or EXCEPT in the question. If you treat the word "LEAST" as one of the details you must satisfy, you have a better chance of understanding what the question is asking. And when you check your answer, make "LEAST" one of the details you check for.

Here's an example of a question that uses the word "EXCEPT."

> If there are exactly 5 times as many children as adults at a show, all of the following could be the number of people at a show EXCEPT
>
> (A) 102
>
> (B) 80
>
> (C) 36
>
> (D) 30

You're looking for the number that *cannot* be the sum of a number plus five times that number. There are several ways to solve this problem ($x + 5x = 6x$), including trial and error. You may also know that all possible numbers must be multiples of 6. The only number that is NOT a multiple of 6 is 80. The answer is (B).

Again, the key to answering these questions correctly is remembering that all of the choices EXCEPT one are actually correct, and that you are looking for the incorrect one.

Be Familiar with Multiple-Choice Question Types

You will probably see more than one question format on a multiple-choice test. Here are examples of some of the more common question formats.

1. Complete the statement

In this type of question, you are given an incomplete statement. You must select the choice that will make the completed statement correct.

> The emergence in the 1960's of movements such as the Black Muslims and the Black Panthers reflected the
>
> (A) continuing support of Black Americans for the goals of Martin Luther King Jr.
>
> (B) failure of federal legislation to satisfy the rising expectations of Black Americans
>
> (C) renewed dedication among Black Americans to work with White liberals toward achieving equality
>
> (D) growing economic power of young Black Americans

To check your answer, reread the question and add your answer choice at the end. Be sure that your choice best completes the sentence.

The correct answer is (B). Civil rights legislation was slow to address the concerns of Black Americans. The Black Panthers were originally formed to patrol black neighborhoods and to protect residents from what Panthers believed were acts of brutality by police. The Black Muslims aimed to create and legitimate a separate social identity for Blacks outside the predominant culture, which they viewed as the creation of a White racist society.

2. *Which of the following*

This question type is discussed in detail on page 87. Also discussed earlier in the chapter are strategies for helping you understand what the question is asking and for understanding details in the question that will help you select the correct choice. Consider this additional example.

> Which of the following groups contains three words that are pronounced differently depending on whether they are used as nouns or verbs?
>
> (A) lick, bottle, can
>
> (B) table, herd, carpet
>
> (C) drive, catalog, board
>
> (D) sow, entrance, present

The question above asks you to choose the group of words that are pronounced one way when they are used as nouns and another way when they are used as verbs. Pronounce these words to yourself to check your answer. (The correct answer is (D).)

3. *Roman numeral choices*

This format is used when there can be more than one correct answer in the list. Consider the following example.

Of the sentences below, which two contain a weak reference?

> I. The principal disapproved of the students' wearing shorts in school.
>
> II. We spent the whole day on a bird-watching expedition, but we didn't see one.
>
> III. Joe found time for his composing whenever he could, but none of his music was ever published.
>
> IV. He was an excellent horseman, but he never owned any.
>
> (A) I and III
>
> (B) I and IV
>
> (C) II and III
>
> (D) II and IV

One useful strategy in this type of question is to assess each possible answer before looking at the answer choices. Then evaluate the answer options. In the question above, sentence II and sentence IV contain weak references (a "weak reference" is a grammatical term that describes a situation in which a pronoun used in a sentence is not clearly linked to the noun to which the pronoun is supposed to refer). So the answer is (D).

4. *LEAST, EXCEPT, NOT*

This question type is discussed at length earlier in the chapter. It asks you to select the choice that doesn't fit. You must be very careful with this question type, because it's easy to forget that you're selecting the negative. This question type is used in situations in which there are several good solutions, or ways to approach something, but also a clearly wrong way to do something.

5. Questions about graphs, tables, or reading passages

The important thing to keep in mind when answering questions about tables, graphs, or reading passages is to answer the question that is asked. In the case of a map or graph, you should consider reading the questions first, and then look at the map or graph in light of the questions you have to answer. In the case of a long reading passage, you might want to go ahead and read the passage, marking places you think are important, and then answer the questions.

Look at this example.

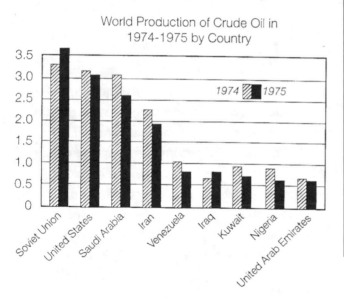

How many of the countries shown in the graph above produced more crude oil in 1975 than in 1974 ?

(A) None

(B) One

(C) Two

(D) Three

There is no reason to spend a great deal of time trying to understand the entire graph in detail when you are being asked a very specific question about it. Here the best approach is to read the question and then look at the graph with the question in mind. You can quickly see that two countries produced more crude oil in 1975 than in 1974, so the answer is (C).

Here is another example.

ESTIMATED POPULATION OF AMERICAN COLONIES, 1630 AND 1750		
	1630	**1750**
New England		
White inhabitants	1,796	349,029
Black inhabitants	0	10,982
Middle Colonies		
White inhabitants	340	275,723
Black inhabitants	10	20,736
Southern Colonies		
White inhabitants	2,450	309,588
Black inhabitants	50	204,702
Total		
White inhabitants	4,586	934,340
Black inhabitants	60	236,420

Which of the following is a correct statement supported by the chart above?

(A) Religion was a powerful force opposing slavery in the American colonies.

(B) Slavery grew rapidly throughout the American colonies despite restrictions on the slave trade.

(C) Southern landholders preferred the labor of indentured servants to slave labor.

(D) By 1750, the southern colonies had become demographically distinct from the other colonies.

As with the question about the graph on the previous page, the best way to approach this question would be to look at the question before studying the table. You might want to look over the table briefly in order to get yourself oriented. (What is it about? How is it organized?) But the key to answering correctly is reading the question and using the table to answer it.

The only claim that is fully supported by the table is (D). No other answer can be drawn solely from this chart.

6. Other Formats

New formats are developed from time to time in order to find new ways of assessing knowledge with multiple-choice questions. If you see a format you are not familiar with, read the directions carefully. Then read and approach the question the way you would any other question, asking yourself what you are supposed to be looking for, and what details are given in the question that help you find the answer.

Useful Facts about the Test

1. **You can answer the sections of the test in any order.** You can go through the questions from beginning to end, as many test takers do, or you can create your own path. Perhaps you will want to answer questions in your strongest field first and then move from your strengths to your weaker areas. There is no right or wrong way. Use the approach that works for you.

2. **There are no trick questions on the test.** You don't have to find any hidden meanings or worry about trick wording. All of the questions on the test ask about subject matter knowledge in a straightforward manner.

3. **Don't worry about answer patterns.** There is one myth that says that answers on multiple-choice tests follow patterns. There is another myth that there will never be more than two questions with the same lettered answer following each other. There is no truth to either of these myths. Select the answer you think is correct, based on your knowledge of the subject.

4. **There is no penalty for guessing.** Your test score is based on the number of correct answers you have, and incorrect answers are not counted against you. When you don't know the answer to a question, try to eliminate any obviously wrong answers and then guess at the correct one.

5. **It's OK to write in your test booklet.** You can work problems right on the pages of the booklet, make notes to yourself, mark questions you want to review later, or write anything at all. Your test booklet will be destroyed after you are finished with it, so use it in any way that is helpful to you.

6. **Bring a calculator.** The questions in the mathematics section will be easier to answer with a calculator, especially one that calculates square roots and percentages. You are allowed to bring a nonprogrammable calculator to the test, and you should. It will be useful for answering some math questions.

Smart Tips for Taking the Test

1. **Put your answers in the right "bubbles."** It seems obvious, but be sure that you are "bubbling in" the answer to the right question on your answer sheet. You would be surprised at how many candidates fill in a "bubble" without checking to see that the number matches the question they are answering.

2. **Skip the questions you find to be extremely difficult.** There are bound to be some questions that you think are hard. Rather than trying to answer these on your first pass through the test, leave them blank and mark them in your test booklet so that you can come back to them. Pay attention to the time as you answer the rest of the questions on the test and try to finish with 10 or 15 minutes remaining so that you can go back over the questions you left blank. Even if you don't know the answer the second time you read the questions, see if you can narrow down the possible answers, and then guess.

3. **Keep track of the time.** Bring a watch to the test, just in case the clock in the test room is difficult for you to see. Remember that, on average, you have one minute to answer each of the 120 questions. One minute may not seem like much time, but you will be able to answer a number of questions in only a few seconds each. You will probably have plenty of time to answer all of the questions, but if you find yourself becoming bogged down in one section, you might decide to move on and come back to that section later.

4. **Read all of the possible answers before selecting one** — and then reread the question to be sure the answer you have selected really answers the question being asked. Remember that a question that contains a phrase like "Which of the following does NOT . . ." is asking for the one answer that is NOT a correct statement or conclusion.

5. **Check your answers.** If you have extra time left over at the end of the test, look over each question and make sure that you have filled in the "bubble" on the answer sheet as you intended. Many candidates make careless mistakes that could have been corrected if they had checked their answers.

6. **Don't worry about your score when you are taking the test.** No one is expected to get all of the questions correct. Your score on this test is not analogous to your score on the SAT, the GRE, or other similar tests. It doesn't matter on this test whether you score very high or barely pass. If you meet the minimum passing scores for your state, and you meet the other requirements of the state for obtaining a teaching license, you will receive a license. Your actual score doesn't matter, as long as it is above the minimum required score. With your score report you will receive a booklet entitled *Understanding Your Praxis Scores,* which lists the passing scores for your state.

Chapter 8
Practice Questions

Practice Questions

Now that you have studied the content topics in the four areas and have worked through strategies relating to multiple-choice questions, you should take the following practice questions. You will probably find it helpful to simulate actual testing conditions, giving yourself about 90 minutes to work on the questions. You can cut out and use the answer sheet provided if you wish.

Keep in mind that the test you take at an actual administration will have different questions, although the proportion of questions in each area and major subarea will be approximately the same. You should not expect the percentage of questions you answer correctly in these practice questions to be exactly the same as when you take the test at an actual administration, since numerous factors affect a person's performance in any given testing situation.

When you have finished the practice questions, you can score your answers and read the explanations of the best answer choices in chapter 9.

THE **PRAXIS**
S E R I E S ™

TEST CODE:

0014

TEST NAME:

Elementary Education:
Content Knowledge

Practice Questions

Four-Function or Scientific Calculator Permitted.

Time—93 Minutes
93 Questions

(Note, at the official test administration, there will be 120 questions,
and you will be allowed 120 minutes to complete the test.)

DO NOT USE INK

Use only a pencil with soft black lead (No. 2 or HB) to complete this answer sheet.
Be sure to fill in completely the oval that corresponds to the proper letter or number.
Completely erase any errors or stray marks.

ETS THE **PRAXIS** SERIES™

Answer Sheet C

PAGE 1

1. NAME

Enter your last name and first initial.
Omit spaces, hyphens, apostrophes, etc.

Last Name (first 6 letters) — F I

(A)(B)(C)(D)(E)(F)(G)(H)(I)(J)(K)(L)(M)(N)(O)(P)(Q)(R)(S)(T)(U)(V)(W)(X)(Y)(Z)

2.

YOUR NAME: (Print)
Last Name (Family or Surname) — First Name (Given) — M. I.

MAILING ADDRESS: (Print)
P.O. Box or Street Address — Apt. # (If any)

City — State or Province

Country — Zip or Postal Code

TELEPHONE NUMBER: ( ) Home — ( ) Business

SIGNATURE:

TEST DATE:

3. DATE OF BIRTH

Month	Day
Jan.	
Feb.	
Mar.	
April	
May	
June	
July	
Aug.	
Sept.	
Oct.	
Nov.	
Dec.	

4. SOCIAL SECURITY NUMBER

(0)(1)(2)(3)(4)(5)(6)(7)(8)(9)

5. CANDIDATE ID NUMBER

(0)(1)(2)(3)(4)(5)(6)(7)(8)(9)

6. TEST CENTER / REPORTING LOCATION

Center Number — Room Number

Center Name

City — State or Province

Country

7. TEST CODE / FORM CODE

(0)(1)(2)(3)(4)(5)(6)(7)(8)(9)

8. TEST BOOK SERIAL NUMBER

9. TEST FORM

10. TEST NAME

Educational Testing Service, ETS, the ETS logo, and THE PRAXIS SERIES:PROFESSIONAL
ASSESSMENTS FOR BEGINNING TEACHERS and its logo are registered trademarks of
Educational Testing Service.

ETS Educational Testing Service

51055 • 08920 • TF71M500
MH01159   Q2573-06

I.N. 202974

1 2 3 4

CERTIFICATION STATEMENT: (Please write the following statement below. DO NOT PRINT.)

"I hereby agree to the conditions set forth in the *Registration Bulletin* and certify that I am the person whose name and address appear on this answer sheet."

_____

_____

_____

SIGNATURE: _____ DATE: _____ / _____ / _____

Month   Day   Year

BE SURE EACH MARK IS DARK AND COMPLETELY FILLS THE INTENDED SPACE AS ILLUSTRATED HERE: ●

#		#		#		#	
1 Ⓐ Ⓑ Ⓒ Ⓓ		41 Ⓐ Ⓑ Ⓒ Ⓓ		81 Ⓐ Ⓑ Ⓒ Ⓓ		121 Ⓐ Ⓑ Ⓒ Ⓓ	
2 Ⓐ Ⓑ Ⓒ Ⓓ		42 Ⓐ Ⓑ Ⓒ Ⓓ		82 Ⓐ Ⓑ Ⓒ Ⓓ		122 Ⓐ Ⓑ Ⓒ Ⓓ	
3 Ⓐ Ⓑ Ⓒ Ⓓ		43 Ⓐ Ⓑ Ⓒ Ⓓ		83 Ⓐ Ⓑ Ⓒ Ⓓ		123 Ⓐ Ⓑ Ⓒ Ⓓ	
4 Ⓐ Ⓑ Ⓒ Ⓓ		44 Ⓐ Ⓑ Ⓒ Ⓓ		84 Ⓐ Ⓑ Ⓒ Ⓓ		124 Ⓐ Ⓑ Ⓒ Ⓓ	
5 Ⓐ Ⓑ Ⓒ Ⓓ		45 Ⓐ Ⓑ Ⓒ Ⓓ		85 Ⓐ Ⓑ Ⓒ Ⓓ		125 Ⓐ Ⓑ Ⓒ Ⓓ	
6 Ⓐ Ⓑ Ⓒ Ⓓ		46 Ⓐ Ⓑ Ⓒ Ⓓ		86 Ⓐ Ⓑ Ⓒ Ⓓ		126 Ⓐ Ⓑ Ⓒ Ⓓ	
7 Ⓐ Ⓑ Ⓒ Ⓓ		47 Ⓐ Ⓑ Ⓒ Ⓓ		87 Ⓐ Ⓑ Ⓒ Ⓓ		127 Ⓐ Ⓑ Ⓒ Ⓓ	
8 Ⓐ Ⓑ Ⓒ Ⓓ		48 Ⓐ Ⓑ Ⓒ Ⓓ		88 Ⓐ Ⓑ Ⓒ Ⓓ		128 Ⓐ Ⓑ Ⓒ Ⓓ	
9 Ⓐ Ⓑ Ⓒ Ⓓ		49 Ⓐ Ⓑ Ⓒ Ⓓ		89 Ⓐ Ⓑ Ⓒ Ⓓ		129 Ⓐ Ⓑ Ⓒ Ⓓ	
10 Ⓐ Ⓑ Ⓒ Ⓓ		50 Ⓐ Ⓑ Ⓒ Ⓓ		90 Ⓐ Ⓑ Ⓒ Ⓓ		130 Ⓐ Ⓑ Ⓒ Ⓓ	
11 Ⓐ Ⓑ Ⓒ Ⓓ		51 Ⓐ Ⓑ Ⓒ Ⓓ		91 Ⓐ Ⓑ Ⓒ Ⓓ		131 Ⓐ Ⓑ Ⓒ Ⓓ	
12 Ⓐ Ⓑ Ⓒ Ⓓ		52 Ⓐ Ⓑ Ⓒ Ⓓ		92 Ⓐ Ⓑ Ⓒ Ⓓ		132 Ⓐ Ⓑ Ⓒ Ⓓ	
13 Ⓐ Ⓑ Ⓒ Ⓓ		53 Ⓐ Ⓑ Ⓒ Ⓓ		93 Ⓐ Ⓑ Ⓒ Ⓓ		133 Ⓐ Ⓑ Ⓒ Ⓓ	
14 Ⓐ Ⓑ Ⓒ Ⓓ		54 Ⓐ Ⓑ Ⓒ Ⓓ		94 Ⓐ Ⓑ Ⓒ Ⓓ		134 Ⓐ Ⓑ Ⓒ Ⓓ	
15 Ⓐ Ⓑ Ⓒ Ⓓ		55 Ⓐ Ⓑ Ⓒ Ⓓ		95 Ⓐ Ⓑ Ⓒ Ⓓ		135 Ⓐ Ⓑ Ⓒ Ⓓ	
16 Ⓐ Ⓑ Ⓒ Ⓓ		56 Ⓐ Ⓑ Ⓒ Ⓓ		96 Ⓐ Ⓑ Ⓒ Ⓓ		136 Ⓐ Ⓑ Ⓒ Ⓓ	
17 Ⓐ Ⓑ Ⓒ Ⓓ		57 Ⓐ Ⓑ Ⓒ Ⓓ		97 Ⓐ Ⓑ Ⓒ Ⓓ		137 Ⓐ Ⓑ Ⓒ Ⓓ	
18 Ⓐ Ⓑ Ⓒ Ⓓ		58 Ⓐ Ⓑ Ⓒ Ⓓ		98 Ⓐ Ⓑ Ⓒ Ⓓ		138 Ⓐ Ⓑ Ⓒ Ⓓ	
19 Ⓐ Ⓑ Ⓒ Ⓓ		59 Ⓐ Ⓑ Ⓒ Ⓓ		99 Ⓐ Ⓑ Ⓒ Ⓓ		139 Ⓐ Ⓑ Ⓒ Ⓓ	
20 Ⓐ Ⓑ Ⓒ Ⓓ		60 Ⓐ Ⓑ Ⓒ Ⓓ		100 Ⓐ Ⓑ Ⓒ Ⓓ		140 Ⓐ Ⓑ Ⓒ Ⓓ	
21 Ⓐ Ⓑ Ⓒ Ⓓ		61 Ⓐ Ⓑ Ⓒ Ⓓ		101 Ⓐ Ⓑ Ⓒ Ⓓ		141 Ⓐ Ⓑ Ⓒ Ⓓ	
22 Ⓐ Ⓑ Ⓒ Ⓓ		62 Ⓐ Ⓑ Ⓒ Ⓓ		102 Ⓐ Ⓑ Ⓒ Ⓓ		142 Ⓐ Ⓑ Ⓒ Ⓓ	
23 Ⓐ Ⓑ Ⓒ Ⓓ		63 Ⓐ Ⓑ Ⓒ Ⓓ		103 Ⓐ Ⓑ Ⓒ Ⓓ		143 Ⓐ Ⓑ Ⓒ Ⓓ	
24 Ⓐ Ⓑ Ⓒ Ⓓ		64 Ⓐ Ⓑ Ⓒ Ⓓ		104 Ⓐ Ⓑ Ⓒ Ⓓ		144 Ⓐ Ⓑ Ⓒ Ⓓ	
25 Ⓐ Ⓑ Ⓒ Ⓓ		65 Ⓐ Ⓑ Ⓒ Ⓓ		105 Ⓐ Ⓑ Ⓒ Ⓓ		145 Ⓐ Ⓑ Ⓒ Ⓓ	
26 Ⓐ Ⓑ Ⓒ Ⓓ		66 Ⓐ Ⓑ Ⓒ Ⓓ		106 Ⓐ Ⓑ Ⓒ Ⓓ		146 Ⓐ Ⓑ Ⓒ Ⓓ	
27 Ⓐ Ⓑ Ⓒ Ⓓ		67 Ⓐ Ⓑ Ⓒ Ⓓ		107 Ⓐ Ⓑ Ⓒ Ⓓ		147 Ⓐ Ⓑ Ⓒ Ⓓ	
28 Ⓐ Ⓑ Ⓒ Ⓓ		68 Ⓐ Ⓑ Ⓒ Ⓓ		108 Ⓐ Ⓑ Ⓒ Ⓓ		148 Ⓐ Ⓑ Ⓒ Ⓓ	
29 Ⓐ Ⓑ Ⓒ Ⓓ		69 Ⓐ Ⓑ Ⓒ Ⓓ		109 Ⓐ Ⓑ Ⓒ Ⓓ		149 Ⓐ Ⓑ Ⓒ Ⓓ	
30 Ⓐ Ⓑ Ⓒ Ⓓ		70 Ⓐ Ⓑ Ⓒ Ⓓ		110 Ⓐ Ⓑ Ⓒ Ⓓ		150 Ⓐ Ⓑ Ⓒ Ⓓ	
31 Ⓐ Ⓑ Ⓒ Ⓓ		71 Ⓐ Ⓑ Ⓒ Ⓓ		111 Ⓐ Ⓑ Ⓒ Ⓓ		151 Ⓐ Ⓑ Ⓒ Ⓓ	
32 Ⓐ Ⓑ Ⓒ Ⓓ		72 Ⓐ Ⓑ Ⓒ Ⓓ		112 Ⓐ Ⓑ Ⓒ Ⓓ		152 Ⓐ Ⓑ Ⓒ Ⓓ	
33 Ⓐ Ⓑ Ⓒ Ⓓ		73 Ⓐ Ⓑ Ⓒ Ⓓ		113 Ⓐ Ⓑ Ⓒ Ⓓ		153 Ⓐ Ⓑ Ⓒ Ⓓ	
34 Ⓐ Ⓑ Ⓒ Ⓓ		74 Ⓐ Ⓑ Ⓒ Ⓓ		114 Ⓐ Ⓑ Ⓒ Ⓓ		154 Ⓐ Ⓑ Ⓒ Ⓓ	
35 Ⓐ Ⓑ Ⓒ Ⓓ		75 Ⓐ Ⓑ Ⓒ Ⓓ		115 Ⓐ Ⓑ Ⓒ Ⓓ		155 Ⓐ Ⓑ Ⓒ Ⓓ	
36 Ⓐ Ⓑ Ⓒ Ⓓ		76 Ⓐ Ⓑ Ⓒ Ⓓ		116 Ⓐ Ⓑ Ⓒ Ⓓ		156 Ⓐ Ⓑ Ⓒ Ⓓ	
37 Ⓐ Ⓑ Ⓒ Ⓓ		77 Ⓐ Ⓑ Ⓒ Ⓓ		117 Ⓐ Ⓑ Ⓒ Ⓓ		157 Ⓐ Ⓑ Ⓒ Ⓓ	
38 Ⓐ Ⓑ Ⓒ Ⓓ		78 Ⓐ Ⓑ Ⓒ Ⓓ		118 Ⓐ Ⓑ Ⓒ Ⓓ		158 Ⓐ Ⓑ Ⓒ Ⓓ	
39 Ⓐ Ⓑ Ⓒ Ⓓ		79 Ⓐ Ⓑ Ⓒ Ⓓ		119 Ⓐ Ⓑ Ⓒ Ⓓ		159 Ⓐ Ⓑ Ⓒ Ⓓ	
40 Ⓐ Ⓑ Ⓒ Ⓓ		80 Ⓐ Ⓑ Ⓒ Ⓓ		120 Ⓐ Ⓑ Ⓒ Ⓓ		160 Ⓐ Ⓑ Ⓒ Ⓓ	

FOR ETS USE ONLY	R1	R2	R3	R4	R5	R6	R7	R8	TR	CS

LITERATURE AND LANGUAGE ARTS

1. Which of the following is an example of internal conflict?

   (A) "All the way home, Emilio felt angry with himself. Why couldn't he have spoken up at the meeting? Why was he always so shy?"

   (B) "Juanita and Marco disagreed about where they should take the money they had found."

   (C) "In the high winds, the crew was barely able to keep the sails from dipping sideways. Each time the wind accelerated, the crew almost lost the boat."

   (D) "Celine struggled to walk through the cold, blowing wind."

Question 2 is based on the following poem.

The fallen leaves are cornflakes
That fill the lawn's wide dish,
And night and noon
The wind's a spoon
That stirs them with a swish.

Excerpted from "December Leaves" in Don't Ever Cross a Crocodile *by Kaye Starbird. Copyright © 1963, 1991 Kaye Starbird.*

2. Which of the following devices or figures of speech appears most frequently in the poem?

   (A) Foreshadowing
   (B) Personification
   (C) Metaphor
   (D) Hyperbole

Questions 3 and 4 are based on the following passage.

We came back to the city Labor Day Monday — us and a couple million others — traffic crawling, a hot day, the windows practically closed up tight to keep Cat in. I sweated, and then cat hairs stuck to me and got up my nose. Considering everything, Pop acted quite mild.

I met a kid up at the lake in Connecticut who had skin-diving equipment. He let me use it one day when Mom and Pop were off sight-seeing. Boy, this has fishing beat hollow! I found out there's a skin-diving course at the Y, and I'm going to begin saving up for the fins and mask and stuff. Pop won't mind forking out for the Y membership, because he'll figure it's character building.

Meanwhile, I'm wondering if I can get back up to Connecticut again one weekend while the weather's still warm, and I see that Rosh Hashanah falls on a Monday and Tuesday this year, the week after school opens. Great. So I ask this kid — Kenny Wright — if I can maybe come visit him that weekend so I can do some more skin diving.

    I. First-person narrative
   II. Use of slang
  III. Use of dialect
  IV. Anthropomorphism

3. The selection contains which of the above?

   (A) I and II only
   (B) II and IV only
   (C) I, III, and IV only
   (D) I, II, III, and IV

4. Which of the following most appropriately describes the narration in the passage?

   (A) It deepens the development of several characters.
   (B) It skips around in time, presenting events in a nonchronological sequence.
   (C) It offers an objective rather than subjective point of view of the events it describes.
   (D) It achieves a casual effect through its nonstandard use of punctuation.

5. While working on a research project, a student uses the Internet and finds a great deal of information on the basic topic chosen. Once the student has gathered this information, the next necessary step in the process of preparing a final report is for the student to

   (A) make a decision about the relevance and reliability of the various pieces of information
   (B) download all the information from the Internet and compile it into a packet for the final report
   (C) decide on a format for the final look of the report
   (D) begin to search for the graphics that will illustrate the final report

German shepherds are the most familiar of the dogs employed as guides for the blind, but collies, boxers, Labrador retrievers, and several other breeds have also been trained successfully. It is not only the dog that must be trained. The blind person who will become the dog's master must also go to a special school, where the two can develop trust and a close understanding.

6. The primary purpose of the passage is to

    (A) describe different breeds of dogs so that people can choose a suitable guide dog
    (B) express an opinion about the preferred breed of dog to work with blind people
    (C) present information about how guide dogs and blind people receive training to work together
    (D) give a detailed explanation of the process for training guide dogs

Although the creative process of screenwriting owes a great deal to the history and development of the theater, the two art forms differ. In a play, the bulk of what is on the page is the characters' dialogue; in a screenplay the balance shifts toward scene description, the actions of the characters, and the visuals the audience sees. Put another way, the play depends upon the words of the characters to carry the weight of the storytelling, while a screenplay (and the film made from it) depends on the actions of the characters.

7. Which of the following organizational strategies is used in the passage?

    (A) Chronological order
    (B) Compare and contrast
    (C) Problem and solution
    (D) Argument and counterargument

Alex baits a hook with his salmon, attaches a heavy sinker, and hangs the line overboard. It drops to the bottom. He waits and feels with his fingers for a tug on the line. He feels a nibble. He pulls. Nothing. He feels another nibble and tugs hard. He's got it. The hook is set. Alex holds on and starts pulling it in.

8. Which of the following is the predominant pattern of organization in the passage?

    (A) Chronological order
    (B) Compare and contrast
    (C) Problem and solution
    (D) Argument and counterargument

9. Which of the following concepts is best supported by current research on emergent literacy?

    (A) Reading and writing develop concurrently and in interrelated ways.
    (B) Literacy learning has distinct beginning and ending points.
    (C) Children begin their literacy learning when they enter school.
    (D) Children begin their literacy learning after having mastered basic letter-sound skills.

Prior to reading a selection about pond life from a science textbook, a teacher asks the students to write all that they know about the topic quickly and spontaneously for about five minutes. Then the teacher asks several students to share their thoughts with the class, either reading verbatim or talking through what they have written. The teacher briefly points out similarities and differences in the students' concepts.

10. The teacher's primary goal in this word exploration activity is to help the students

   (A) establish stronger peer relationships by encouraging the use of a common vocabulary to describe experiences
   (B) develop students' speaking and listening skills in a particular content area
   (C) read a text assignment smoothly and quickly when they come to it
   (D) expand their schemata and knowledge structures to help them construct meaning and retain information

Ba-room, ba-room, ba-room, baripity, baripity, baripty, baripty — Good. His dad had the pickup going. He could get up now. Jess slid out of bed and into his overalls. He didn't worry about a shirt because once he began running he would be hot as popping grease even if the morning air was chill, or shoes because the bottoms of his feet were by now as tough as his worn-out sneakers.

11. The passage above contains characteristic elements of which of the following literary genres?

   (A) Autobiography
   (B) Realistic fiction
   (C) Fable
   (D) Folktale

Once upon a time, a beggar woman went to the house of a poor peasant and asked for something to eat. The peasant's wife gave her some bread and milk. When she had eaten it, she took a barley-corn out of her pocket, and said —" This will I give thee; set it in a flowerpot, and see what will come out of it."

The woman set the barley-corn in an old flowerpot, and the next day the most beautiful plant had shot up, which looked just like a tulip, but the leaves were shut close together, as if it still were in bud . . .

12. Which of the following elements is displayed by the passage?

   (A) Simple characterization and quickly moving action
   (B) Thematic emphasis on differences between the rich and the poor
   (C) A richly described setting
   (D) A melancholy tone

A cat came fiddling out of a barn,
With a pair of bag-pipes under her arm;
She could sing nothing but, Fiddle cum fee,
The mouse has married the humble-bee.
Pipe, cat; dance, mouse;
We'll have a wedding at our good house.

13. The rhythm and rhyme of this selection is most typical of a

   (A) poem in free verse
   (B) nursery rhyme
   (C) limerick
   (D) fairy tale

Questions 14-16 are based on the following chart.

WILDFLOWERS

Name	Native Region	Appearance	Soil	Light	Blooms
Arroyo lupine	Western United States	Bluish-purple flower spikes	Best in heavy clay soil	Full sun	April-May
Blue flax	California	Small, blue flowers with pale centers covering the loosely spreading plant	Likes dry, light, sandy soil	Full sun	May-September
California bluebell	The arid Southwest	Deep, royal blue bell-shaped flowers	Needs well-drained, dry, sandy, relatively poor soil	Full sun	February-June
California poppy	The arid Southwest	Brilliant orange cup-shaped flowers	Prefers light, sandy soil; tolerates drought	Full sun	April-August
Five spot	California	White flowers with a vivid dark purple spot at the outer tip of each petal	Tolerates wide range of soil conditions	Full sun to light shade	March-May
Texas paintbrush	Texas	Single erect stem bearing bright orange bracts with a tiny, pale yellow flower in the center	Well-drained areas; tolerates drought	Full sun	April-June
Tidy-Tips	California and Southwest desert	Yellow flowers fringed in white	Very dry, well-drained soil	Full sun	March-May

14. According to the chart, which of the following pairs of wildflowers would be well suited for sandy soil and full sun and would be in bloom during the month of July?

   (A) California bluebell and Five spot
   (B) Blue flax and Five spot
   (C) California poppy and California bluebell
   (D) Blue flax and California poppy

15. According to the chart, which wildflower is a spreading plant that requires full sun and is native to California?

   (A) Blue flax
   (B) California poppy
   (C) Five spot
   (D) Tidy-Tips

16. According to the chart, which wildflower requires full sun and produces bluish blooms for less than three months a year?

   (A) Arroyo lupine
   (B) Blue flax
   (C) California bluebell
   (D) Tidy-Tips

"Three people I knew in school have recently became known for their roles as actors in Hollywood movies."

17. Which of the following types of usage in the sentence above needs correction?

    (A) Subject-verb agreement
    (B) Pronoun-antecedent agreement
    (C) Verb tense form
    (D) Adjective form

"The Italian restaurant that recently reopened"

18. Which of the following sentences integrates the above sentence fragment into a correct complex sentence?

    (A) The Italian restaurant that recently reopened continuing in the same tradition of fine Italian food.
    (B) The Italian restaurant that recently reopened continues in the same tradition of fine Italian food.
    (C) The Italian restaurant that recently reopened and that continues in the same tradition of fine Italian food.
    (D) The Italian restaurant that recently reopened; it is continuing in the same tradition of fine Italian food.

    Semifinal
    Nonnegotiable
    Prehistoric

19. The three words above have in common which of the following characteristics?

    (A) They are all superlative adjectives.
    (B) They all derive from related Latin roots.
    (C) They all have multiple meanings.
    (D) They all contain prefixes.

"It took the young child a long time to lick the <u>mile-high</u> ice-cream cone."

20. The underlined word in the sentence is an example of

    (A) a simile
    (B) personification
    (C) hyperbole
    (D) an oxymoron

A word can have multiple meanings and be used as different parts of speech in different contexts. For example, the word "hollow" has three meanings, each of which is a different part of speech.

hol • low

1 *n.* low-lying land; small depression in a flat surface.
2 *adj.* empty, with nothing inside.
3 *v.* to hollow out; to make something hollow.

21. Which of the following sentences uses "hollow" as a noun, that is, the first definition in the list above?

    (A) Ashley's hollow features displayed her disappointment over losing her pet.
    (B) Lilly's footsteps echoed with a hollow sound as she entered the old general store.
    (C) Marsha's sheep were grazing in the wide hollow between the mountains.
    (D) Jack's camera captured the raccoons trying to hollow out an old log.

22. Which of the following statements is best supported by current research on language learning for students learning English as a new language?

    (A) Instruction is most beneficial to students of the new language when it is delivered consistently according to a single instructional strategy.
    (B) Teaching students explicitly how to use learning strategies shows surprisingly little correlation with the students' success in learning the new language.
    (C) Students need large amounts of meaning-focused practice of the new language in addition to appropriate form-focused instruction. ✓
    (D) Students of English as a new language learn the language most effectively in an environment with little social interaction to distract them. ✗

I YmHsalm.

---

23. A child wrote this when asked to write "I was at my house and saw a little mouse." The child's work indicates that he or she most likely does NOT fully grasp which of the following concepts?

    (A) There are a number of letter-sound combinations in most words.
    (B) Print is made up of letters.
    (C) Letters have both upper and lower cases.
    (D) Letters stand for sounds in words.

While working on a writing assignment, a student asks a peer to listen to her reading of the rough draft and to offer suggestions for clarifying, expanding, or condensing parts of the draft.

24. The student is engaged in which stage of the writing process?

    (A) Proofreading
    (B) Outlining
    (C) Revising
    (D) Publishing

coat = COET	right = RITE
cool = COL	bought = BAUGHT
curl = CRL	hitch = HICH

25. This sample analysis of a student's spelling test indicates that the student is most likely at which of the following stages of spelling development?

    (A) Representing words with random letters that have no letter-sound correspondence
    (B) Representing words phonetically, with a single letter representing each sound
    (C) Recognition that words are made up of letter patterns that represent sounds
    (D) Knowledge of simple sound-letter correspondence, with no grasp of consonant combinations

An elementary school teacher has been using a variety of activities in the classroom to help her students develop their listening skills. Today's activity requires the students to listen while the teacher reads the directions aloud twice. The first time the students hear the directions, they listen carefully but do not make any marks on their paper. As they listen the second time, they draw certain shapes and lines on their paper in a particular pattern. After the students have finished drawing, they listen while the teacher reads the directions aloud again. They assess their work against the directions and make any corrections that are necessary. As a follow-up activity, they write a reflection on their performance of this activity.

26. The teacher uses this activity to help the students learn how to

   (A) understand another person's point of view
   (B) interpret the beliefs behind a speaker's message
   (C) use sensory acuity to gather information from body language
   (D) attend to oral directions in order to complete a task

MATHEMATICS

27. Which of the following numbers is least?

   (A) 0.103
   (B) 0.1041
   (C) 0.1005
   (D) 0.11

28. The Statue of Liberty casts a shadow 37 meters long at the same time that a vertical 5-meter pole nearby casts a shadow that is 2 meters long. The height, in meters, of the Statue of Liberty is within which of the following ranges?

   (A) 115 m to 120 m
   (B) 105 m to 110 m
   (C) 90 m to 95 m
   (D) 60 m to 65 m

29. In a certain year, 5 percent of the 2,800 employees of a company had a perfect attendance record. Which of the following computations can be used to determine the number of employees with a perfect attendance record?

   (A) $\dfrac{1}{40} \times 2,800$

   (B) $\dfrac{1}{20} \times 2,800$

   (C) $\dfrac{1}{5} \times 2,800$

   (D) $5 \times 2,800$

30. A storeowner buys canvas bags at a cost of 3 for $8.40 and sells them at a price of 5 for $29.00. How many bags must the storeowner sell to make a profit of $1,200 ?

    (A) 60
    (B) 240
    (C) 400
    (D) 600

31. All of the following are equivalent to dividing 288 by 24 EXCEPT

    (A) $(288 \div 4) \div 6$
    (B) $2(144 \div 24)$
    (C) $(144 \div 12) + (144 \div 12)$
    (D) $(240 \div 24) + (48 \div 24)$

Question 32 is based on the following list.

Cheese	$1.19
Milk	$1.63
Juice	$1.99
Cereal	$1.19
Bananas	$0.97
Melon	$0.99
Peaches	$0.61
Bread	$1.39
Butter	$0.89

32. If a shopper purchases the items in the list above at the prices indicated, the change from a $20 bill would be most nearly equal to which of the following? (Assume there is no tax.)

    (A) $7
    (B) $8
    (C) $9
    (D) $10

33. Cindy and Danny have volunteered to start work at the local food bank at 9:00 A.M. every Saturday. It takes 30 minutes to go from Danny's house to the food bank. Cindy picks up Danny, but it takes her 15 minutes to get to Danny's house. If it takes Cindy 45 minutes to get ready in the morning, at what time should she start getting ready?

    In order to solve the problem above, which of the following methods would be most appropriate?

    (A) Use an equation
    (B) Look for a pattern
    (C) Use a graph
    (D) Work backward

34. The sum of a certain two numbers is 7 and the difference of the two numbers is 3. What is the product of these two numbers?

    (A) 8   (B) 10   (C) 12   (D) 14

35. There are 36 students in the photography club at the local high school. If there are half as many boys as girls in the club, how many girls are in the club?

    (A) 30   (B) 24   (C) 18   (D) 12

$$15(4 + 3) = 15 \times 4 + 15 \times 3$$

36. The equation above demonstrates which of the following?

    (A) The distributive property of multiplication over addition
    (B) The commutative property of multiplication
    (C) The associative property of multiplication
    (D) Additive inverse and additive identity

37. The Clearbrook Elementary Wildcats scored an average of 77 points in four games. In the first three games, they scored 70, 76, and 82 points. How many points did they score in their last game?

    (A) 70
    (B) 76
    (C) 77
    (D) 80

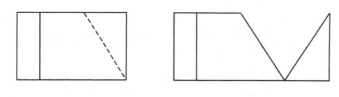

Figure I   Figure II

38. The rectangular region shown in Figure I is cut along the dotted line and reassembled as shown in Figure II. Which of the following statements about the area and perimeter of Figure I and Figure II is true?

    (A) The area of Figure I is equal to the area of Figure II, and the perimeter of Figure I is equal to the perimeter of Figure II.
    (B) The area of Figure I is equal to the area of Figure II, and the perimeter of Figure II is greater than the perimeter of Figure I.
    (C) The area of Figure I is greater than the area of Figure II, and the perimeter of Figure I is greater than the perimeter of Figure II.
    (D) The area of Figure I is greater than the area of Figure II, and the perimeter of Figure I is equal to the perimeter of Figure II.

39. On Greg's map, 1 inch represents 30 miles, and on Lori's map, 1 inch represents 20 miles. The area of a 1-inch by 1-inch square represents how many more square miles on Greg's map than on Lori's map?

    (A) 100
    (B) 250
    (C) 400
    (D) 500

40. In triangle *ABC*, the measure of angle *A* is 47° and the measure of angle *B* is 53°. What is the measure of angle *C*?

    (A) 53°
    (B) 80°
    (C) 90°
    (D) 100°

41. Bill went to sleep at 9:57 P.M. and awoke the next morning at 6:28 A.M. How long did he sleep?

    (A) 9 hr 31 min
    (B) 9 hr 25 min
    (C) 8 hr 31 min
    (D) 8 hr 25 min

**EXPORTS OF COUNTRIES *A*, *B*, AND *C*
TO THE UNITED STATES
(1995-1997)**

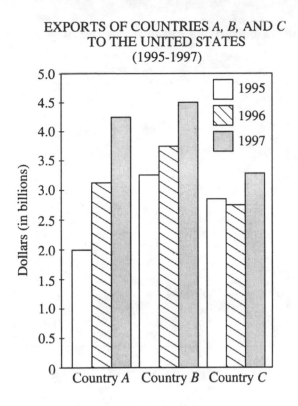

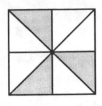

43. The figure above represents a square dartboard. What is the approximate probability that a dart that lands on the board will land in one of the shaded regions?

(A) 0.25
(B) 0.30
(C) 0.38
(D) 0.50

$160	$80	$230	$215	$180
$220	$170	$220	$300	$185

42. Which of the following statements can be inferred from the graph above?

  I. For each country shown, exports to the United States increased each year from the previous year.

  II. The country that had the greatest yearly exports to the United States for each of the years shown had a three-year export total of approximately $12 billion.

  III. The exports of Country A to the United States more than doubled from 1995 to 1997.

(A) I and II only
(B) I and III only
(C) II and III only
(D) I, II, and III

44. Jake researched the prices of ten cameras. The list of prices appears above. He wants to buy a camera for the average price of those ten cameras. How much does Jake want to pay for his camera?

(A) $185
(B) $196
(C) $200
(D) $215

HISTORY AND SOCIAL STUDIES

45. What major geographic feature in North America separates the rivers and streams that flow toward the Pacific Ocean from those that flow toward the Atlantic Ocean?

(A) Appalachian Mountains
(B) Continental Divide
(C) Great Plains
(D) San Andreas Fault

Question 46 refers to the following map.

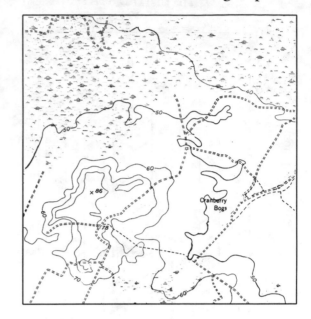

46. What do the solid lines on the map above represent?

(A) Levels of snow accumulation
(B) Lines above which certain trees do not grow
(C) Elevation of land above sea level
(D) The advance of glaciers in the region

Question 47 refers to the following map.

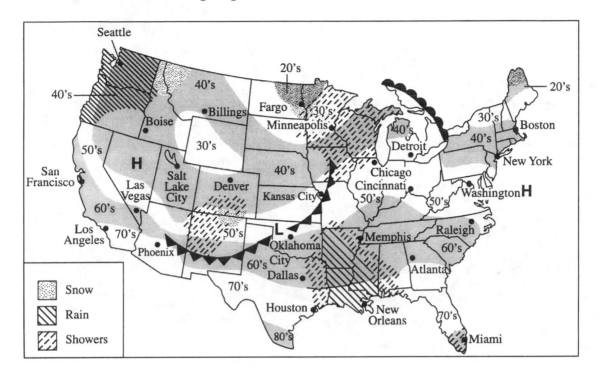

47. Based on the information in the weather map above, which of the following best describes the weather in Minneapolis on this particular day?

   (A) Rain; temperatures in the 30's
   (B) Rain; temperatures in the 40's
   (C) Showers; temperatures in the 30's
   (D) Showers; temperatures in the 40's

48. Which of the following is a known result of volcanic activity?

   (A) An increase in the ozone concentration in the upper atmosphere
   (B) Acid rain in the Arctic regions
   (C) Accelerated desertification in lava-damaged zones
   (D) Temporary cooling of the world's climate

49. During the twentieth century, urbanization and technological advances led to which of the following changes in farming in the United States?

   (A) More farms and more farmers
   (B) More farms and fewer farmers
   (C) Fewer farms and more farmers
   (D) Fewer farms and fewer farmers

50. Which of the following has been a primary cause of soil depletion in deforested rain forest environments?

   (A) The overuse of harmful pesticides
   (B) The introduction of cash-crop agriculture
   (C) Contamination by industrial waste
   (D) The use of chemical fertilizers

51. All of the following contribute to global warming in a significant way EXCEPT

   (A) exhaust from trucks and automobiles
   (B) runoff from pesticides used in agriculture
   (C) deforestation of the rain forest
   (D) burning of fossil fuels to create electricity

Questions 52 and 53 are based on the following map.

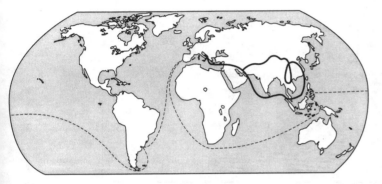

52. Which of the following explorers led the expedition represented by the dotted line on the map?

   (A) Ferdinand Magellan
   (B) Christopher Columbus
   (C) Hernán Cortés
   (D) Juan Ponce de León

53. Which of the following explorers made the voyage represented by the solid line on the map?

   (A) Amerigo Vespucci
   (B) Vasco da Gama
   (C) Marco Polo
   (D) Henry Hudson

54. The development of agriculture and the domestication of animals in the Agricultural Revolution (ca. 10,000–6,000 B.C.E.) led to the establishment of small communities. All of the following were characteristic of these early communities EXCEPT

   (A) settlement around areas of fertile soil
   (B) systems of protection, defense, and government
   (C) division of labor
   (D) systems of written record keeping

55. The holy scriptures for the Islamic faith are called the

   (A) Torah
   (B) Upanishads
   (C) Ramayana
   (D) Koran

56. After the death of Alexander the Great in 323 B.C.E., the major cities of Macedonia, Persia, and Egypt attested to the continuing strong influence of Greek culture by

   (A) closing down trade routes to India after areas of India conquered by Alexander were returned to the original rulers
   (B) raising money to have the life of Alexander immortalized in a series of large statues
   (C) maintaining their laws, language, calendar, and coinage according to Greek systems
   (D) successfully eradicating all indigenous religious traditions

57. In 1517 Martin Luther posted a list of 95 theses on the doors of the cathedral in Wittenberg, Germany. His action led directly to what major episode in European history?

    (A) The Renaissance
    (B) The Reformation
    (C) The Enlightenment
    (D) The Crusades

58. In the decade of the 1990's, after the fall of communism in the Soviet Union, which of the following became widespread in Russia?

    (A) United States popular culture, including American rock music
    (B) Efficient train systems based on West Germany's infrastructure
    (C) New public buildings based on modern architectural ideas, replacing older historical structures
    (D) An unprecedented appreciation for the visual arts, including the construction of several major new museums

59. The principal source of opposition to the ratification of the Constitution during the years 1787–1788 came from a fear that ratification would

    (A) lead to a large national debt
    (B) weaken the power of the states
    (C) put an end to majority-rule among United States citizens
    (D) be the first step in the establishment of a monarchy

60. Which of the following best describes the *Monroe Doctrine,* promulgated by President Monroe in 1823 ?

    (A) A publication from the first Continental Congress that outlined Federalist principles
    (B) The first plan for self-government adopted in the English colonies
    (C) A document designed to end European colonization in the Western Hemisphere
    (D) One of the first documents to oppose slavery in the United States

61. Which of the following happened as an early consequence of the building of the Panama Canal?

    (A) Naturalists took successful steps to preserve unique Central American habitats.
    (B) The nation of Panama took over control and operation of the canal.
    (C) Doctors developed drugs to combat malaria and yellow fever.
    (D) Engineers developed technology to build railroads in mountainous areas.

62. Rosa Parks' actions on the evening of December 1, 1955, in Montgomery, Alabama, constituted a protest against segregation in

    (A) the public transportation system
    (B) the school system
    (C) restaurants and public accommodations
    (D) law enforcement units

63. Which of the following is most closely associated with the philosophy of *The Articles of Confederation* adopted in 1777?

   (A) States' rights
   (B) Manifest Destiny
   (C) Nationalism
   (D) Checks and balances

64. Which of the following statements is true of the United States Congress?

   (A) It writes and passes national laws.
   (B) It interprets laws in the process of deciding issues before the courts.
   (C) It appoints justices and grants pardons.
   (D) It establishes and maintains public schools.

65. Which of the following is guaranteed by the Bill of Rights of the United States Constitution?

   (A) Absolute freedom for the individual
   (B) Protection of the individual from unfair actions by the federal government
   (C) The precedence of individual rights over community rights
   (D) Protection of all individuals from being owned by another individual

66. The President of the United States appoints which of the following?

   (A) The president of the United States Senate
   (B) The vice president of the United States
   (C) State supreme court judges
   (D) Federal appellate court judges

67. Some scholars criticize the use of the term "melting pot" to characterize the history of the American immigrant experience. These scholars believe that the term fails to suggest the extent to which most immigrants

   (A) became assimilated swiftly into American society
   (B) came to the United States for economic reasons
   (C) experienced hardships in the United States
   (D) maintained their native identities and customs in the United States

Question 68 refers to the following list.

   1. Stone, metal, and shell tools and how advanced they were
   2. Burial customs
   3. Number and variety of domesticated animals
   4. Number and variety of domesticated plants
   5. Size-comparisons of various houses
   6. Distribution of artifacts in various excavated houses

68. An anthropologist is interested in determining whether a certain prehistoric society had a large or a small degree of differentiation among social classes. If the anthropologist could examine only three kinds of evidence from the list above, what combination of three would be most helpful?

   (A) 1, 2, 6
   (B) 1, 3, 4
   (C) 2, 3, 4
   (D) 2, 5, 6

69. Cognitive psychology is a theoretical perspective that focuses on

    (A) mental and emotional disorders in humans
    (B) human perception, thought, and memory
    (C) human behavior and how it is shaped by its consequences
    (D) mental states such as self-concept and self-esteem

70. In which of the following job markets in the United States did the number of workers decline during the years 1990–1999 ?

    (A) Service
    (B) Communication
    (C) Manufacturing
    (D) Teaching

71. An increase in the price of home heating oil during an unusually cold winter exemplifies which of the following economic principles?

    (A) Recession
    (B) Private property rights
    (C) Supply and demand
    (D) Price controls

72. In a free-enterprise economy, what is the intended relationship between government and business?

    (A) The government interferes relatively infrequently in the way private businesses operate.
    (B) The government distributes natural resources to businesses.
    (C) The government sets production levels and prices for major industries only.
    (D) The government promotes large businesses at the expense of small, local enterprises.

73. Which of the following is the largest source of federal revenue in the United States?

    (A) Social Security taxes
    (B) Corporate income taxes
    (C) Estate taxes
    (D) Individual income taxes

74. Which of the following best describes the composition of the labor force?

    (A) Everyone over the age of 16 who is actually working
    (B) Everyone over the age of 16 who is capable of working
    (C) Everyone over the age of 16 who is actually working or available for employment and seeking work
    (D) Everyone younger than 62 who is working or available for employment and seeking work

SCIENCE

"As altitude increases, atmospheric pressure decreases, but not at a constant rate."

75. Which of the following graphs best represents this relationship?

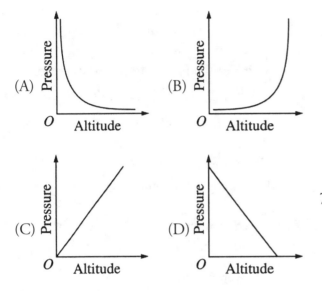

Question 76 refers to the following model.

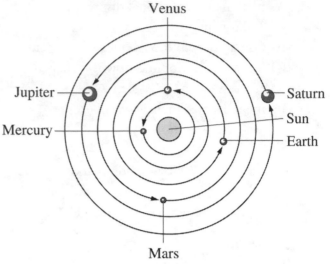

76. A model of the solar system is shown above. Which of the following is LEAST accurately shown in the model?

(A) The relative distance of each planet from the Sun

(B) The order of the planets from nearest to the Sun to farthest from the Sun

(C) The direction of the planetary orbits

(D) The shapes of the planetary orbits

77. A rock picked up on a hillside was found to contain tiny pieces of seashells. Which of the following is the best explanation of how this rock was formed?

(A) It was formed when sediments sank to the bottom of an ancient sea and were subjected to great pressure for long periods of time.

(B) It was formed on or near Earth's surface from magma or lava that flowed during a volcanic eruption.

(C) It was formed when minerals deep inside Earth were subjected to great heat and pressure.

(D) It was formed by seafloor spreading and erosion of the midocean ridge deep in the ocean.

POSSIBLE OUTCOMES FOR TRAIT X

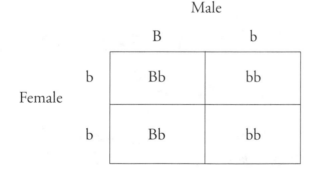

78. Trait X results when B (a dominant gene) is inherited. According to the figure above, what is the probability that an offspring of a male with gene-pair Bb and a female with gene-pair bb will inherit the gene for trait X?

(A) $\frac{1}{4}$

(B) $\frac{2}{4}$

(C) $\frac{3}{4}$

(D) $\frac{4}{4}$

79. Which of the following statements best describes what is most likely to occur in a small hibernating animal when the surrounding air temperature drops slightly below freezing?

(A) The animal will die.

(B) The animal's heart rate and breathing rate will increase.

(C) The animal will shiver, wake up, and then find food high in fat calories.

(D) The rate at which the animal consumes its body fat will increase.

80. Regulating the temperature of the human body is a primary function of which of the following organs?

(A) The lungs

(B) The skin

(C) The liver

(D) The heart

"Ancestors of modern giraffes stretched their necks to reach higher twigs. This eventually caused their offspring to be born with longer necks."

81. Which of the following most accurately describes the statement above?

(A) It is a good example of a species evolving within an isolated, rapidly changing environment.

(B) It is a good example of how natural selection favors a trait that aids survival.

(C) It is a misconception, because organisms cannot pass along acquired characteristics genetically.

(D) It is a misconception, because improved diet rather than muscle movement usually leads to feeding-related traits such as longer necks.

82. Which of the following statements best describes, in a simplified way, what occurs during the process of respiration in plants?

   (A) Plants use energy, water, and carbon dioxide to produce sugar and oxygen.
   (B) Plants use sugar and oxygen to produce energy, water, and carbon dioxide.
   (C) Plants use water and oxygen to produce sugar and carbon dioxide.
   (D) Plants use water, sugar, and carbon dioxide to produce oxygen and energy.

"The earth's vegetation is part of a web of life in which there are intimate and essential relations between plants and the earth, between plants and other plants, between plants and animals."

83. This passage is from *Silent Spring* (1962), by Rachel Carson, a book about the destructive effects of DDT. Carson's "web of life" refers to which of the following scientific concepts?

   (A) Food chain
   (B) Evolution
   (C) Ecosystem
   (D) Extinction

84. Which of the following does NOT describe a chemical change?

   (A) Silver tarnishing when exposed to air
   (B) Ice melting when heated
   (C) Lemon juice turning brown when heated
   (D) Iodine solution becoming purple in the presence of starch

$$6CO_2 + 6H_2O \rightarrow C_6H_{12}O_6 + 6O_2$$

85. According to the model above for photosynthesis, a molecule of glucose (sugar) contains how many atoms of carbon?

   (A) One
   (B) Two
   (C) Six
   (D) Twelve

86. A spaceship is on its way to the Moon. While on a space walk outside the spaceship, an astronaut claps her hands together. Which of the following best explains why the astronaut hears no sound?

   (A) There is no matter in space in which sound can be transmitted.
   (B) The frequency of sound waves produced in space are too high to be heard by the human ear.
   (C) Without Earth's magnetic field, sound waves cannot be transmitted.
   (D) The solar wind interferes destructively with sound waves, canceling them out.

87. Which of the following is an example of heat transfer by radiation?

   (A) A spoon in a hot drink gets hot.
   (B) Water in a pot on an electric burner boils.
   (C) The air in a store near the hot asphalt of a parking lot becomes warmer.
   (D) The Sun heats Earth's surface.

88. Which of the following is an example of a net force of zero acting on an object?

   (A) A truck accelerating down a hill
   (B) A girl kicking a ball
   (C) A book sitting on a table
   (D) A parachuter jumping out of an airplane

89. A simple controlled experiment is pictured above. What is the variable in the experiment?

(A) Sponge
(B) Sunflower seeds
(C) Water
(D) Dish

Question 90 refers to the following list.

1. Analyze the issue
2. Gather information
3. Make a decision
4. Take action

90. According to the Science-Technology-Society (S-T-S) problem-solving steps above, which of the following would be an example of the step "Take action"?

(A) Two students interview an expert on composting and discuss the issue of whether people in a residential area should be encouraged to convert green yard waste into fertilizer.
(B) A mother and a son brainstorm about the role of decomposers in an ecosystem and the causes of environmental conflicts between neighbors.
(C) A father and a daughter make a compost bin in a corner of their backyard that will convert yard waste into soil fertilizer.
(D) After reading articles on the subject, a class develops a chart showing arguments that either support or oppose composting.

91. Antibiotics are chemicals that are capable of inhibiting the growth of certain bacteria. Which of the following diseases CANNOT be successfully treated with an antibiotic?

(A) Strep throat
(B) Tuberculosis
(C) Tetanus
(D) Influenza

92. The theory of continental drift, first proposed by Alfred Wegener in 1912, has been refined by which of the following theories?

(A) Plate tectonics
(B) Evolution
(C) The big bang
(D) Paleomagnetism

"Measuring the breathing rates of hibernating animals requires the same fundamental rigor as measuring the strength of hurricanes."

93. The statement above illustrates which of the following concepts?

(A) Most classification systems used by scientist are based on the same logic.
(B) Focus on function and structure can be found across the scientific spectrum.
(C) Studying phenomena in their own environment is critical to successful scientific observation.
(D) Some scientific procedural schemes are important across all scientific fields.

END OF PRACTICE TEST

Chapter 9
Right Answers and Explanations
for the Practice Questions

▶ ▶ ▶ ▶ ▶ ▶ ▶ ▶ ▶ ▶ ▶ ▶

Right Answers and Explanations for the Practice Questions

Now that you have answered all of the practice questions, you can check your work.
Compare your answers with the correct answers in the table below.

Question Number	Correct Answer	Content Category
1	A	Understanding Literature
2	C	Understanding Literature
3	A	Understanding Literature
4	B	Understanding Literature
5	A	Understanding Literature
6	C	Text Structures and Organization in Reading and Writing
7	B	Text Structures and Organization in Reading and Writing
8	A	Text Structures and Organization in Reading and Writing
9	A	Literacy Acquisition and Reading Instruction
10	D	Literacy Acquisition and Reading Instruction
11	B	Literacy Acquisition and Reading Instruction
12	A	Literacy Acquisition and Reading Instruction
13	B	Literacy Acquisition and Reading Instruction
14	D	Literacy Acquisition and Reading Instruction
15	A	Literacy Acquisition and Reading Instruction
16	A	Literacy Acquisition and Reading Instruction
17	C	Language in Writing
18	B	Language in Writing
19	D	Language in Writing
20	C	Language in Writing
21	C	Language in Writing
22	C	Language in Writing
23	A	Communication Skills
24	C	Communication Skills
25	C	Communication Skills
26	D	Communication Skills
27	C	Number Sense Numeration
28	C	Number Sense Numeration
29	B	Number Sense Numeration
30	C	Number Sense Numeration
31	C	Number Sense Numeration
32	C	Number Sense Numeration
33	D	Number Sense Numeration
34	B	Algebraic Concepts
35	B	Algebraic Concepts
36	A	Algebraic Concepts
37	D	Algebraic Concepts
38	B	Informal Geometry and Measurement
39	D	Informal Geometry and Measurement
40	B	Informal Geometry and Measurement
41	C	Informal Geometry and Measurement
42	C	Data Organization and Interpretation
43	C	Data Organization and Interpretation
44	B	Data Organization and Interpretation
45	B	Geography
46	C	Geography
47	C	Geography
48	D	Geography
49	D	Geography
50	B	Geography
51	B	Geography
52	A	World History
53	C	World History
54	D	World History
55	D	World History
56	C	World History
57	B	World History
58	A	World History
59	B	U.S. History
60	C	U.S. History
61	C	U.S. History
62	A	U.S. History
63	A	Political Science
64	A	Political Science
65	B	Political Science
66	D	Political Science
67	D	Anthropology, Sociology, Psychology
68	D	Anthropology, Sociology, Psychology
69	B	Anthropology, Sociology, Psychology
70	C	Economics
71	C	Economics
72	A	Economics
73	D	Economics
74	C	Economics
75	A	Earth Science
76	A	Earth Science
77	A	Earth Science
78	B	Life Science
79	D	Life Science
80	B	Life Science
81	C	Life Science
82	B	Life Science
83	C	Life Science
84	B	Physical Science
85	C	Physical Science
86	A	Physical Science
87	D	Physical Science
88	C	Physical Science
89	C	Science as Inquiry
90	C	Science in Personal and Social Perspectives
91	D	Science in Personal and Social Perspectives
92	A	History and Nature of Science
93	D	Unifying Processes

Explanations of Right Answers

LITERATURE AND LANGUAGE ARTS

1. This question asks you to recognize an example of a particular literary element. Internal conflict is a struggle between opposing forces in the mind of a single character. (A) is the only choice where conflict is taking place in the mind of a character; accordingly, (A) is the correct answer.

2. This question asks you to apply your knowledge of figures of speech. A metaphor is a figure of speech that vividly describes a thing by identifying it directly with something else (for example, in line 4, "The wind's a spoon"). In line 1, the poet identifies fallen leaves with cornflakes. In line 2, the poet identifies the lawn with a wide dish. In line 4, the poet identifies the wind with a spoon. Therefore (C) is the correct answer.

3. This question asks you to apply your knowledge of narrative, structural, and stylistic elements to the selection. The narrator constantly says "I," and so the selection is written in first-person narrative. The narrator also uses slang (for example, "this has fishing *beat hollow*!" and "forking out for the Y membership"). There is no particular dialect represented, nor is the cat in the passage portrayed anthropomophically — that is, as having human qualities. The correct answer, therefore, is (A).

4. This question asks you to apply your knowledge of narrative elements to the selection. The first paragraph takes place in the past; the beginning of the second paragraph leaps back before the action of the first paragraph; the last part of the second paragraph glides into the present and future; and the third paragraph moves between past and future events. There is some character development in the narrator, but not much at all in other characters mentioned. The selection is subjective (reflecting the narrator's somewhat quirky point of view) rather than objective. The punctuation in the passage is standard. The correct answer, therefore, is (B).

5. This question asks you to apply your knowledge of good research techniques. After a student has located and accessed information, it is necessary to analyze, interpret, and evaluate that information for its usefulness and reliability before synthesizing it. Choices (B), (C) and (D) skip the next logical step of evaluating the information for usefulness and relevance, and move ahead to the aspects of presenting a final product. The correct answer is (A).

6. This question asks you to identify the main purpose of the nonfiction passage. Some passages are intended to entertain, others to argue for a point of view, and others to convey information. In this passage, the author is conveying information, not arguing for a point of view about the dogs, describing different breeds, or explaining the training process in any detail. Choice (C), therefore, best describes the primary purpose of the passage — to inform the reader by presenting facts.

7. This question asks you to recognize a type of textual organization. In the first sentence above, the author notes how screenwriting and playwriting are similar. In the next two sentences, the author contrasts the two, focusing on a crucial difference between them. Therefore (B) is the correct answer.

8. This question asks you to recognize the predominant pattern of text structure. The writer organizes events in the order in which they happened, that is, in chronological order, using simple descriptive language to help the reader visualize the process. Therefore (A) is the correct answer.

9. This question asks you to recognize current research conclusions related to emergent literacy. Emergent literacy is the idea that children grow into reading and writing with no real beginning or ending point, that reading and writing develop concurrently and in interrelated ways, and that this learning process starts long before children enter school and does not depend on mastery of letter-sound skills. The correct answer is (A).

10. This question asks you to put together the given example of "word exploration" with the intended influences of this strategy in the classroom. The approach would not be used primarily to establish peer relationships, develop speaking or listening skills, or improve in reading fluency. The strategy helps develop or activate the students' knowledge-schema about a topic in order to help them in constructing meaning and retaining information as they learn about the topic. Therefore (D) is the correct answer.

11. This question asks you to apply your knowledge of genres of literature, matching a representative selection with its genre. Realistic fiction is imaginative writing that accurately reflects life as it has been lived in the past or could be lived today. It consists of a prose narrative with a plot that unfolds through the actions, speech, and thoughts of the characters. In this selection, the main character (Jess) is just waking up and getting dressed — a story is about to unfold. An autobiography typically is not written in third person, as this selection is. Realistic and fairly current details like noisy sneakers are not characteristic elements of fables or folktales. The correct answer, therefore, is (B).

12. This question asks you to recognize structural and stylistic elements characteristic of a particular genre, the fairy tale. In this selection, the action moves very quickly, and the characters are developed with a minimum of description. None of the other choices accurately describes what is going on in this passage. The correct answer is (A).

13. This question asks you to recognize typical characteristics of a nursery rhyme. Nursery rhymes are verses traditionally told or sung to small children. They are characterized by a lively and slightly unpredictable meter, regular rhyme schemes, playful and nonsense situations, and nonsense words. The correct answer, therefore, is (B).

14. This question and the next two questions ask you to use information in a table to come to correct conclusions. Usually when you encounter a map, graph, chart, or other visual representation, all of the information you need to answer the question is found in the visual. When answering sets of questions like this

one, you will probably find it helpful to read the questions first, and then go back to the visual, instead of trying to absorb all the information in the visual first. In this question you need to find the two wildflowers that have information in the Soil, Light, and Blooms columns matching the conditions referred to in the question. The correct answer is (D).

15. The correct answer is (A).

16. The correct answer is (A).

17. This question asks you to apply your knowledge of basic grammar to a sentence that contains a single error in usage. The "present perfect" form of the verb "to become" is "have become," not "have became" as found in the sentence. Therefore, the correct answer is (C).

18. This question asks you to use your knowledge of the construction of a complex sentence. The given sentence fragment contains a subordinate adjective clause ("that recently reopened") that cannot stand on its own to complete the sentence begun by "The Italian restaurant". When the fragment "the Italian restaurant that recently opened" is combined with the continuation in (B), the result is a correct complex sentence. Choices (A) and (C) are still sentence fragments. Choice (D) is an incorrectly formed sentence attempt. (B) is the correct answer.

19. This question asks you to recognize a basic concept relating to the structure and origin of words, that is, that many English words are combinations of several word elements. In this example, all of the words feature a prefix: "semi," "non," and "pre." The correct answer, therefore, is (D).

20. This question asks you to apply your knowledge of figurative language or figures of speech. Since the ice-cream cone is most likely only a few inches high, not a mile high, the writer has effectively used hyperbole. Hyperbole is defined as "an extravagant exaggeration used for emphasis or effect." The correct answer is (C).

21. This question asks you to figure out a word's meaning in context. The word "hollow" can be used as a noun, adjective, or verb with different meanings. A skillful reader can usually use the context to figure out which meaning and part of speech is intended in a given sentence. In choices (A) and (B), "hollow" is used as an adjective. In choice (D), "hollow" is used as a verb. Choice (C) is the only choice in which hollow is used as a noun. Therefore (C) is the correct answer.

22. The question asks you to recognize a major trend in current research surrounding new-language learning. Current research suggests that when English learners receive instruction with explicit teaching of *learning strategies,* the learners become more efficient and effective learners in the second language. Teachers also need to be open to a multitude of learning styles among the learners in the classroom and present instruction in many different ways. Students need large amounts of meaning-focused practice of the language along with form-focused instruction at appropriate times. They actually improve their new language skills significantly during most social interaction. The correct answer, therefore, is (C).

23. This question asks you to analyze a child's work and make an interpretation of the child's understanding of basic concepts of written communication. Notice that this is a NOT

question, indicating that you are looking for the one concept the child seems not to understand. The child has not yet realized that a number of letter-sound combinations make up most words, and he or she has instead appears to use one letter to represent either one whole word or several words. The correct answer, therefore, is (A).

24. This question asks you to recognize an example of an activity associated with a particular stage in the writing process. The example describes a student who is asking for help in examining the ideas, structure, and expression in her draft. This is part of the "Revising" stage, making (C) the correct answer.

25. This question asks you to analyze a student's work and make an interpretation of the child's stage in spelling development. The student has progressed through the random-letter stage, the simple phonetic stage, and the stage where students rely on single letters to represent combinations of consonants. The student's spelling of "coat" ("COET"), "bought" ("BAUGHT"), "right" ("RITE"), and "hitch" ("HICH") indicates that he or she recognizes that there are letter-patterns to represent single sounds. The correct answer, therefore, is (C).

26. This question asks you to interpret a description of a lesson activity and match it to the type of listening skills it is intended to build. Listening skills encompass a wide range of skills, including all of the skills appearing in the four choices. However, the activities described above focus on a speaker giving instructions, with the students listening to and following those instructions. The correct answer, therefore, is (D).

MATHEMATICS

27. This question tests your knowledge of decimal values. Without the decimal, 1041 would be the greatest number and 11 would be the least, but because these are decimals, the position in relation to the decimal point is crucial in determining the value. It is helpful to work from left to right to determine which number is least. In this case, 0.1005 is the least number, and (C) is the correct answer. Another way to approach this kind of problem is to add a zero to the end of 0.103 in (A), and two zeroes to the end of 0.11 in (D) so that all four choices represent so many ten-thousandths. This does not change the numbers' values, but makes it easier to determine that (D) is the greatest, being equal to 1,100 ten-thousandths, and (C) is the least, being equal to 1,005 ten-thousandths. Again, (C) is the correct answer.

28. This question can be solved by setting up a proportion. The ratio between the height of the Statue of Liberty and the length of its shadow is equal to the ratio between the height of the pole and the length of its shadow. The proportion will look like this (where L represents the height of the Statue of Liberty):

$$\frac{L}{37} = \frac{5}{2}$$

Multiplying both sides by 37 and then simplifying both sides of the equation gives you $L = 92.5$m. Note that other proportions can be set up, such as: Statue height *(L)* divided by pole height (5 meters) equals statue shadow length (37 meters) divided by pole shadow length (2 meters). This will also give the correct result. Therefore, (C) is the correct answer.

29. This question tests your facility with fractions, percentages, and decimals and your ability to recognize equivalents among them. 5 percent means 5 one-hundredths (0.05) or 5 divided by 100 $\left(\dfrac{5}{100}\right)$, which reduces to $\dfrac{1}{20}$. In mathematics, the word "of" means "multiply." So, to obtain an answer for 5 percent of 2,800 employees, it is necessary to multiply 2,800 by either 0.05 or by $\dfrac{1}{20}$. (B) is the correct answer.

30. This question tests your ability to set up mathematical computations to solve a real-world problem. The storeowner's cost to buy one bag is 8.40 ÷ 3 = 2.80. The price at which a single bag sells for is 29.00 ÷ 5 = 5.80. So the profit for one bag is 5.80 − 2.80 = 3. Finally, the number of bags needed to make a $1,200 profit is 1,200 ÷ 3 = 400. Therefore, (C) is the correct answer.

31. This question tests your knowledge of the order of operations in basic computations. Notice that this is an EXCEPT question, which means that you are looking for the single choice that is not equivalent. Operations within the parentheses must be solved before operations outside the parentheses. That is, the parentheses group together the equations that should be solved first. If you divide 288 by 24, the result is 12. Each of the choices also equals 12 except (C), which equals 24. Therefore, (C) is the correct answer.

32. This question tests simple addition and subtraction or estimation and rounding. You can add the prices of the groceries with your calculator and get a total of $10.85, leaving $9.15 when you subtract from $20.00. Alternatively, you can perform the calculation in your head by rounding up or down to the nearest dollar and/or by finding pairs of prices that nearly equal rounded dollar amounts. The correct answer is (C).

33. This question tests your ability to identify the most appropriate strategy for solving a real-world problem. In this case, the most appropriate strategy is to start at 9:00 A.M. and work backward: 8:30 A.M. — arrive at Danny's; 8:15 A.M. — leave for Danny's house; 7:30 A.M. — start getting ready. The answer, therefore, is (D).

34. This question can be solved using basic algebra by letting x and y represent the two numbers. The following two equations represent the information given:

$$x + y = 7$$
$$x - y = 3$$

When these two equations are added, the result is $2x = 10$. Divide each side by 2 to get $x = 5$. Substitute 5 back into either equation for x and obtain $y = 2$. The product of 5 and 2 is 10, making (B) the correct answer. You could also use a more basic method. The choices for numbers whose sum is 7 are 7 + 0, 6 + 1, 5 + 2, and 4 + 3. Of these, only 5 and 2 give a difference of 3. The product of 5 and 2 is 10, again making (B) the correct answer.

35. This question can be solved using basic algebra. If g is used to represent the number of girls, the number of boys would be $0.5g$. The following equation can be solved for g:

$$.5g + g = 36$$
$$1.5g = 36$$
$$g = 24$$

To solve this without using algebra, you can reason that since there are half as many boys as girls in the club, three equal groups of students will consist of two all-girl groups and one all-boy group. Because 36 students divided by 3 groups equals 12, the two all-girl groups equal a total of 2 times 12, or 24 girls.

$$\text{Girls} + \text{Girls} + \text{Boys} = 36$$
$$12 + 12 + 12 = 36$$
$$24 + 12 = 36$$

The correct answer is (B).

36. This question asks you to identify a basic algebraic property. The distributive property of multiplication over addition means that each term within the parentheses is multiplied by the number outside the parentheses. The products are then added together.

$$A(B + C) = AB + AC$$

The answer is (A).

37. This question tests your knowledge of an average (or arithmetic mean) and your ability to set up and solve several computations. An average of 77 points in four games means that they scored a total of 77 times 4, or 308, points. Since the scores for the first three games are given as 70, 76, and 82 points, it is necessary to add these up (228 points) and subtract from the four-game total of 308 points. This leaves 80 points for the last game's score. The answer is (D).

38. This question tests your knowledge of "area" and "perimeter" and asks you to compare two related figures. Since the two figures are composed of exactly the same subparts, their areas are equal because area does not change

with rearrangement. But perimeter can change, and Figure II features the hypotenuses of the two triangles on the perimeter, each of which contributes additional length to the perimeter of Figure II. The correct answer, therefore, is (B).

39. This question asks you to apply your ability to calculate area using standard real-world miles on a map. Area is a two-dimensional representation of a surface (length times width, base times height, etc.). A 1-inch by 1-inch square on Greg's map represents a square 30 miles on each side. The area of this square is 30 miles multiplied by 30 miles, or 900 square miles. On Lori's map, the 1-inch by 1-inch square represents a square 20 miles on each side. The area of this square is 20 miles multiplied by 20 miles, or 400 square miles. The difference between these is 500 square miles. (D) is the correct answer.

40. This question tests your knowledge of the basic fact that the three angles of any triangle total 180 degrees and asks you to apply that fact to find the measure of a particular angle. Angle A (47 degrees) and angle B (53 degrees) add up to 100 degrees. Subtract the total of these two angles from 180 degrees to get 80 degrees, the measure of angle C. The correct answer is (B).

41. This question tests your ability to calculate with standard units of time. Bill slept for 3 minutes from 9:57 P.M. until 10:00 P.M. and for 2 hours from 10:00 P.M. until 12:00 P.M. (midnight). Then he slept another 6 hours and 28 minutes until 6:28 A.M. This adds up to a total of 8 hours and 31 minutes. The correct answer is (C).

42. This question asks you to read and interpret a bar graph. Note that the scale is in billions of dollars and rises in increments of $0.5 billion. The exports from Country *C* decreased a small amount from 1995 to 1996, so statement I cannot be inferred from the graph. Statements II and III can be inferred, since Country *B* had the greatest yearly exports, for a three-year total of nearly $12 billion. Also, the exports from Country *A* more than doubled, going from $2 billion to just over $4 billion. The correct answer is (C).

43. This question tests your knowledge of simple probability. The shaded region represents 3 out of a total of 8 equal regions on the dartboard. This means that a dart has a 3 out of 8 chance of landing in a shaded region, or a probability of 3/8 (0.375), which rounds to 0.38. Probabilities in mathematics range from 0 (no chance) to 1 (100% chance). The correct answer is (C).

44. This question tests your knowledge of how to compute an "average" and apply it to a real-world situation. The average (or arithmetic mean) is found by adding all the measurements together and dividing the total by the number of measurements involved. Here the ten measurements add up to a total of $1,960. Divide this figure by 10 to get an average of $196. The correct answer is (B).

HISTORY AND SOCIAL STUDIES

45. This question tests your knowledge of important geographic features of North America. The Continental Divide is the series of mountain ridges extending from Alaska to Mexico that forms the watershed of North America. Most of the Divide runs along peaks of the Rocky Mountains. In the United States, it is often called the Great Divide. The correct answer, therefore, is (B).

46. This question asks you to identify the purpose of a feature in a common topological map. This kind of map has contour lines, one line for each major level of elevation. All the land at the same elevation is connected by a line. These lines often form circles or ovals—one inside the other. If contour lines are very close together, the surface is steep. If the lines are spread apart, the land is flat or rises very gradually. The correct answer is (C).

47. This question asks you to interpret a map, using its legends and markings to identify specific information. Minneapolis is found in the northern plains, west of the Great Lakes, a region of the country showing showers (slanted broken lines). The alternating shaded and clear bands representing temperature show that Minneapolis is located at the edge of the clear band marked 30 degrees. Thus, there are showers and temperatures in the 30's in Minneapolis for the day represented on the map, and (C) is the correct answer.

48. This question asks you to use your knowledge of volcanic activity and its effects. Of the four choices, only (D) is caused by volcanoes. Volcanic activity produces huge amounts of dust in the atmosphere that may have a cooling effect by reflecting the sunlight into space and keeping it from warming Earth. A recent example is the 1991 eruption of Mt. Pinatubo in the Philippines. The summer of 1992 was exceptionally cool. (D) is the correct answer.

49. This question asks you to apply your knowledge about how farming in the United States has changed over the last one hundred years. Although population growth has necessitated more food, there are fewer but much larger farms in the United States and fewer people who identify themselves as farmers. Large conglomerates run most farms now, using advanced technology. The correct answer, therefore, is (D).

50. This question tests your knowledge of the effects of human activity on rain forest environments. The primary cause of soil depletion after deforestation has been cattle ranching and the raising of cash crops that are not suitable for the soil. The crops deplete the soil's fertility after a year or two. The correct answer, therefore, is (B).

51. This question asks you to recognize the human activities that do and do not contribute significantly to global warming. Note that this is an EXCEPT question, asking you to choose the single activity among the choices that does not contribute in a major way. Industries and vehicles that burn fossil fuels are the main source of the chemicals that are gradually warming Earth's atmosphere. Deforestation increases the levels of carbon dioxide in the atmosphere. (Carbon dioxide is one of the main "greenhouse gases.") Pesticides used in agriculture do not contribute to formation of the greenhouse gases that raise temperatures on Earth. The correct answer, therefore, is (B).

52. These two questions test your knowledge of the major voyages of discovery. The expedition led by Ferdinand Magellan, whose route is represented by the dotted line on the map, was the first in history to sail around the world (1519–1522), although Magellan himself failed to complete the journey, having been killed in the Philippines in 1521. The answer is (A).

53. Marco Polo (1254–1324) made a famous voyage to China in the late 1200's. The solid line represents Marco Polo's voyage, making (C) the correct answer.

54. This question asks you to recognize major characteristics of early settlements in the period of the Agricultural Revolution. Note that this is an EXCEPT question, which means you are looking for the single choice that is *not* characteristic. The Agricultural Revolution moved humans from the nomadic, hunter-gathering life to a more settled existence, which in turn required finding fertile land to use, simple systems of defense and government, and more specialization in labor. Written record keeping, however, came later with the growth of cities and urban centers (ca. 5,000–3,000 B.C.E.). The correct answer, therefore, is (D).

55. This question asks you to recall an important basic fact, the name of the central scriptures of the Islamic faith. The Koran (also spelled as "Qur'an") is the correct answer, (D).

56. This question asks you to identify the influence of Alexander the Great's conquests. The cities that had been part of his empire had come to focus mainly on trade. City officials adapted their laws, language, calendar, and coins along Greek models. Greek customs and ideas were brought into the schools, and Greek methods of business were used by bankers and merchants. Indigenous religious traditions persisted throughout the period of continuing Greek cultural influence. The correct answer, therefore, is (C).

57. This question asks you to connect the name of a major European movement with the person and action that sparked it. Luther decided to take a public stand against the actions of a friar named Tetzel. Tetzel was raising money to rebuild St. Peter's Cathedral in Rome by selling indulgences (pardons) for sins. Luther was troubled by Tetzel's tactics and attacked the "pardon merchants" in his theses. His actions began the Reformation movement for religious reform, which led to the founding of what would later become known as the "Protestant" denominations. The Crusades had taken place several hundred years before Luther, while in most places in Europe the Renaissance was well under way before Luther posted his theses on the cathedral door. The Enlightenment would not take place until the 1700's. The correct answer, therefore, is (B).

58. This question taps your knowledge of twentieth-century transformations in world history. In the 1990's, after the fall of communism in the Soviet Union, cultural imports such as rock music from the United States became extremely popular. During that decade there were no major advances in the train systems, no major museums were built,

nor were older buildings torn down and replaced in significant numbers. The correct answer, therefore, is (A).

59. This question tests your knowledge of the political debates and ideas in the early years of the United States. The Constitution was a highly controversial document and required several years before it was finally drafted and ratified. Those who supported the Constitution's strengthening of the national federal government were called Federalists. Those who opposed it were called Anti-Federalists. One of the Anti-Federalists' great worries was that the independence and sovereignty of individual states would be eroded. The correct answer is (B).

60. This question tests your knowledge of major ideas and documents during the period of growth and expansion of the United States. The *Monroe Doctrine* was written in 1823 by Secretary of State John Quincy Adams and was made American policy by then-President James Monroe. While the United States would not interfere with any existing European colonies in the Americas, Monroe declared it would oppose any new ones. North and South America "are henceforth not to be considered as subjects for future colonization by any European powers." The correct answer is (C).

61. This question tests your knowledge of the basic events surrounding the building of the Panama Canal in 1904–1914. Early on in the project, many workers died from yellow fever. Dr. William Gorgas traced the spread of the disease to mosquitoes and ordered the nearby swamps and ponds drained to prevent mosquitoes from multiplying. Within two years, yellow fever had disappeared. (C) is the correct answer.

62. This question tests your knowledge of important events in the Civil Rights movement of the 1950's and 1960's in the United States. Ms. Parks' refusal to give up her bus seat to a white man sparked the Montgomery bus boycott, which led to the emergence of Martin Luther King, Jr. and his rise to leadership in the civil rights cause. The correct answer is (A).

63. This question tests your knowledge of the key documents and ideas that were part of the founding of the United States. The *Articles,* America's first constitution, provided for a new central government to which the states surrendered little of their power. For the states, the Confederation was "a firm league of friendship" in which each state retained "its sovereignty, freedom and independence." The correct answer is (A).

64. This question tests your knowledge of the United States government and the duties and responsibilities of each of the three branches. The judicial branch interprets laws, and the executive branch appoints justices and grants pardons. Each state government has a department of education, which sets up rules and standards for the public schools in the state. It is the responsibility of the Senate and House of Representatives, together constituting the legislative branch of the United States government, to write and pass national laws. The correct answer is (A).

65. This question tests your knowledge of the key contents and ideas in the foundational documents of the United States government. While the Bill of Rights (1791) protects individuals from unfair actions of the federal government, it does not guarantee absolute freedom. An individual's rights are limited when they conflict with the rights of others and the safety and health of the community. The Bill of Rights did not abolish slavery. The correct answer is (B).

66. This question tests your knowledge of the United States government and the duties and responsibilities of each of the three branches. Of the four choices, only federal appellate court judges are appointed by the President. The correct answer is (D).

67. This question tests your knowledge of an important phrase, "melting pot," and asks you to choose the reason why some scholars object to it. Today in the United States, there are neighborhoods where people speak a language other than English. Many of the people in these neighborhoods still follow the way of life of their homelands or the homelands of their parents, grandparents, and great-grandparents, which suggests to some scholars that ethnic differences do not quickly "melt" away. The correct answer is (D).

68. This question asks you to draw on your knowledge of basic anthropological inquiry methods and select the kinds of evidence that would be most helpful in determining how social status worked in a particular society. Social status would be most evident in phenomena in which all people in the society participated. All people were buried; all lived in shelters. Different burials for different people would indicate a differentiation in status. Different sizes of houses, and differences in kinds and numbers of artifacts in different houses would also indicate a social differentiation. The presence of particular types of tools, animals, and plants provide

good evidence for some questions about a society, but not the question of social status. The correct answer is (D).

69. This question tests your knowledge of basic theoretical approaches in the field of psychology. Choice (A) describes the focus of abnormal psychology. Behavioral psychology's focus is summarized in choice (C). Mental states, in (D), relate most closely to the perspective of humanistic psychology. Choice (B) summarizes cognitive psychology's focus and is the correct answer.

70. This question tests your knowledge of recent economic and labor trends. Manufacturing jobs declined during this period as service and information industries and teaching opportunities grew. The correct answer is (C).

71. This question asks you to apply your knowledge of basic economic principles to a real-life situation. The cold winter increases the demand for home heating oil at a time when the availability of oil (or "supply") does not proportionately increase. The price of the oil is likely to increase then because the demand increases and the supply does not. The correct answer is (C).

72. This question asks you to recognize a basic characteristic of free-enterprise systems. Free enterprise stresses freedom of individual economic practice and a free market based on supply and demand. In command economies (which for some time prevailed in Eastern Europe), the means of production are publicly owned and economic activity is controlled by a central authority. Yet even in societies that rely on free enterprise, government action has been required to curb free enterprise's abuses (monopolies and fraud, for example). The correct answer is (A).

73. This question tests your knowledge of the economics of the United States government. The pie chart below shows the major sources of the government's revenue.

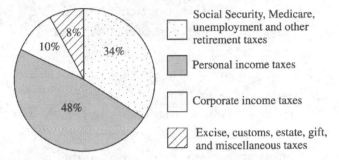

The correct answer, therefore, is (D).

74. This question tests your knowledge of how labor statistics are derived. People are classified as being in the labor force in the United States if they are 16 years old or older and if they are employed, unemployed, or in the Armed Forces during the survey week. People not counted in the labor force are those who are going to school full-time, keeping house, retired, unable to work because of long-term physical or mental illness, or who have, for other reasons, not been seeking employment. The correct answer is (C).

SCIENCE

75. In this question, you are asked to interpret graphs and match the correct graph with a relationship expressed in words. (B) and (C) are wrong, because they show that as altitude increases (i.e., left to right), pressure *increases* rather than decreases. (D) is wrong, because, although pressure does decrease (i.e., high to low), the relationship is linear and therefore *constant* rather than not constant. (A) shows that as altitude increases pressure decreases,

but not at a constant rate: the degree of decrease gets smaller as altitude increases. The correct answer, therefore, is (A).

76. This question asks you to put together your knowledge of the solar system with a simple model representing part of the solar system. Models such as this are often found in textbooks, and it is important to distinguish what each model represents well and what each one represents poorly. In this model, the order of the planets going outward from the Sun is correct, as is the direction of the planetary orbits. The shapes of the planetary orbits are represented by circles. While the orbits are actually elliptical, the eccentricities of most of the orbits are so small that they are nearly circular. Even in a correctly scaled diagram, the small elongations of the orbits may not be discernable, thus the circular representation is close to being accurate. The relative distance of each planet from the Sun is inaccurate, since the inner four planets are significantly more closely spaced than the two outer planets shown. The correct answer, therefore, is (A).

77. This question asks you to apply your knowledge of rock formation and the processes of Earth's history to a single sample, a rock containing tiny pieces of seashells. The presence of seashells in a rock on a hillside indicates that the hillside was under water many years ago. During the time that the ancient sea existed, shells, which are the "houses" of sea creatures, would have fallen to the seabed when the animals died. The pressure of the water over very long periods of time would have compacted and cemented the shells and sediment into rocks that later were exposed when the sea dried up. The correct answer, therefore, is (A).

78. This question asks you to use your understanding of genetics and your ability to read a simple genetic table (Punnett square) to arrive at a probability level for a particular set of conditions. The table shows that the offspring will inherit one of four possible pairs of genes. There are two chances out of four that an offspring could inherit gene B, the gene for trait X. The probability is therefore $\frac{2}{4}$, or $\frac{1}{2}$, making the correct answer (B).

79. This question asks you to identify the effect of one condition (air temperature) on an organism with hibernation capacities. Hibernation is a state of winter dormancy associated with lowered body temperature and lowered metabolism. Hibernating animals "go to sleep" mainly because there is not enough food in their environment to feed them over the winter. During hibernation, an animal's heartbeat and breathing rate slow down and its body temperature falls almost to that of its surroundings. Animals use hardly any energy and can survive on the food stored as fat in their bodies. The correct answer, therefore, is (D).

80. This question asks you to recognize which organ in the human body is chiefly responsible for the function of regulating the body's temperature. The correct answer is (B), since it is the skin that performs temperature regulation through the activation of sweat glands.

81. This question asks you to recognize a common misconception about evolution. It was once thought that an organism's acclimation to the environment could be passed on to its offspring. This was called the "inheritance of acquired characteristics." This theory, however, is now known to be wrong. Only genetically determined traits can be passed on to offspring. The correct answer, therefore, is (C).

82. This question tests your knowledge of a basic definition. During respiration in plants, the organic compound sugar is broken down to produce energy, and water and carbon dioxide are by-products of the process. The correct answer, therefore, is (B).

83. This question asks you to interpret a passage about science and connect it to an important scientific concept. Rachel Carson was concerned that the chemical pesticides introduced by humans into the environment would have a devastating effect on the interconnected webs that all life-forms on Earth are part of. Carson referred to the work of researchers who found that many birds and wild mammals retained considerable quantities of DDT in their bodies and that this DDT could be found in natural food chains. That is, plant pesticides had a devastating effect on animals because the animals were dependent on the plant life in that environment. This relationship is an example of "ecosystem," an ecological community together with its environment, functioning as a unit. (C), therefore, is the correct answer.

84. This question asks you to recognize examples of chemical changes. Note that this is a "NOT" question, so you will be looking for the single choice that is *not* an example of a chemical change. A chemical change occurs when elements react with each other in such a way as to form chemical compounds that have properties and applications very different from their elemental raw materials. (A), (C), and (D) are examples of chemical changes. A new compound is formed that is different from the raw material before the change. (B) is an example of matter changing phase but not changing chemically. When ice melts, it changes phase from a solid to a liquid. (B), therefore, is the correct answer.

85. This question asks you to read a model of a chemical process and correctly find a piece of information within the model. The given model tells us that during photosynthesis 6 molecules (or units) of carbon dioxide combine with 6 molecules of water to produce 1 molecule of sugar and 6 molecules of oxygen. If we examine the sugar molecule, we see that it contains 6 atoms of carbon, 12 atoms of hydrogen, and 6 atoms of oxygen. (C), therefore, is the correct answer.

86. This question asks you to apply your understanding of the fundamental physics of sound to a hypothetical situation. On Earth, the action of two objects hitting each other causes the molecules of air near them to vibrate. Like on the surface of a pond of water after a rock is thrown into it, the vibration travels outward from the source. This is called a sound wave. When the sound wave reaches the ear, the vibration of the air causes the eardrum to vibrate at the same frequency as the frequency of the vibrating source. Without air (or another transmitting medium made of matter), however, there can be no creation, transmission, or reception of sound. The correct answer, therefore, is (A).

87. This question asks you to use your knowledge about the various ways heat can be transferred in order to recognize an example of heat transfer by radiation. (A) is an example of heat transfer by conduction, in which objects in contact are at different temperatures and heat flows from the warmer points to the cooler points. (B) and (C) are examples of heat transfer by convection (in which circulation of currents in a gas or liquid such as air or water transfers the heat from one region to another). (D), the correct answer, is an example of heat transfer by radiation, in which invisible infrared radiation travels from one object to another, carrying energy in the process.

88. This question asks you to select the appropriate example of a net force of zero acting on an object. Newton's second law of motion states that a net force on an object causes the object to accelerate, or change velocity. Therefore, no net force can be acting on an object if it is at rest or moving at constant velocity. A zero net force can be created when two forces of equal size are acting on the object in opposite directions, thus canceling each other out. All of the choices involve acceleration except the book sitting on the table. In this case the force of gravity downward is balanced by the force the table exerts on the book upward, and the book remains at rest. The correct answer, therefore, is (C).

89. This question asks you to apply your knowledge of controlled experimentation to the simple experiment shown in the question. Using a "control" sample and an experimental sample, the scientist changes a single condition (called a "variable") between the two. In the above experiment, all the variables are the same (dish, seeds, sponge) except that the sponge is dry in the control sample and wet in the experimental sample. Thus, the difference between the two is water, making (C) the correct answer.

90. This question asks you to recognize an example of a particular stage in the problem-solving process. According to the S-T-S problem-solving method, taking action involves having a solution to a problem and an action plan that identifies things that can be done in order to get the solution accepted by others. Choices (A), (B), and (D) are examples of gathering information and analyzing the issues, but not examples of making or implementing an action plan. The correct answer, therefore, is (C).

91. This question asks you to recognize the agents at work in major human diseases and identify the one that is *not* bacteria related. Strep throat, tuberculosis, and tetanus are all caused by bacteria, and antibiotics are capable of killing or inhibiting the growth of those bacteria. Influenza (the flu) is a viral disease and thus cannot be successfully treated with an antibiotic. The correct answer, therefore, is (D).

92. This question asks you to link a significant scientific theory from the past with a more recent theory that expands and refines it. Alfred Wegener theorized that the continents once all fit together and drifted apart to their present locations. His theory was rejected by his contemporaries until work in the 1960's found evidence supporting the motion of continents. Today, Earth scientists believe that Earth's surface is made of "plates," thin brittle slabs of crust that interact with the mantle below the crust. These interactions produce movement of continents, earthquakes, volcanoes, mountains, and the crust itself. The correct answer, therefore, is (A).

93. This question asks you to interpret a statement and choose the concept it represents. The statement focuses on a common procedural scheme ("measuring") that is critical for a life science example and an Earth science example. Although classification systems, function, structure, and contextual observation are important concepts, they are not illustrated by the statement. The correct answer, therefore, is (D).

Chapter 10

Are You Ready? Last-Minute Tips

▶ ▶ ▶ ▶ ▶ ▶ ▶ ▶ ▶ ▶ ▶ ▶

Checklist

❏ Do you know the testing requirements for your teaching field in the state(s) where you plan to teach?

❏ Have you followed all of the test registration procedures?

❏ Do you know the topics that will be covered in each test you plan to take?

❏ Have you reviewed any textbooks, class notes, and course readings that relate to the topics covered?

❏ Do you know how long the test will take and the number of questions it contains? Have you considered how you will pace your work?

❏ Are you familiar with the test directions and the types of questions for your test?

❏ Are you familiar with the recommended test-taking strategies and tips?

❏ Have you practiced by working through the practice test questions at a pace similar to that of an actual test?

❏ If constructed-response questions are part of your test, do you understand the scoring criteria for these items?

❏ If you are repeating a test, have you analyzed your previous score report to determine areas where additional study and test preparation could be useful?

The Day of the Test

You should have ended your review a day or two before the actual test date. And many clichés you may have heard about the day of the test are true. You should

- Be well rested

- Take photo identification with you

- Take a supply of well-sharpened No. 2 pencils (at least three)

- Eat before you take the test

- Be prepared to stand in line to check in or to wait while other test takers are being checked in

You can't control the testing situation, but you can control yourself. Stay calm. The supervisors are well trained and make every effort to provide uniform testing conditions, but don't let it bother you if the test doesn't start exactly on time. You will have the necessary amount of time once it does start.

You can think of preparing for this test as training for an athletic event. Once you've trained, and prepared, and rested, give it everything you've got. Good luck.

Appendix A
Study Plan Sheet

▶ ▶ ▶ ▶ ▶ ▶ ▶ ▶ ▶ ▶ ▶ ▶

Study Plan Sheet

See Chapter 1 for suggestions on using this Study Plan Sheet.

STUDY PLAN						
Content covered on test	How well do I know the content?	What material do I have for studying this content?	What material do I need for studying this content?	Where could I find the materials I need?	Dates planned for study of content	Dates completed

Appendix B
For More Information

▶ ▶ ▶ ▶ ▶ ▶ ▶ ▶ ▶ ▶ ▶ ▶

Educational Testing Service offers additional information to assist you in preparing for The Praxis Series™ Assessments. *Tests at a Glance* and the *Registration Bulletin* are both available without charge (see below to order). You can also obtain more information from our Web site: **www.ets.org/praxis**.

General Inquiries

Phone: (800) 772-9476 or (609) 771-7395 (Monday-Friday, 8:00 A.M. to 7:45 P.M., Eastern time)
Fax: (609) 771-7906

Extended Time

If you have a learning disability or if English is not your primary language, you can apply to be given more time to take your test. The *Registration Bulletin* tells you how you can qualify for extended time.

Disability Services

Phone: (866) 387-8602 or (609) 771-7780
Fax: (609) 771-7906
TTY (for deaf or hard-of-hearing callers): (609) 771-7714

Mailing Address

ETS—The Praxis Series
P.O. Box 6051
Princeton, NJ 08541-6051

Overnight Delivery Address

ETS—The Praxis Series
Distribution Center
225 Phillips Blvd.
Ewing, NJ 08628-7435

Please take a moment to complete this review of the Elementary Education: Content Knowledge Study Guide. We appreciate your feedback.

1. Overall, how helpful did you find this study guide?

Very helpful	Somewhat helpful	Neutral	Somewhat unhelpful	Very unhelpful
☐	☐	☐	☐	☐

2. Please rank the different chapters of the study guide in order of helpfulness. Write a **1** next to the most helpful chapter, a **2** next to the second most helpful chapter, and so on.

    _____ Ch. 1: Introduction and Suggestions for Using this Study Guide
    _____ Ch. 2: Background Information of The Praxis Series™ Assessments
    _____ Ch. 3: Language Arts and Reading: Study Topics
    _____ Ch. 4: Mathematics: Study Topics
    _____ Ch. 5: Social Studies: Study Topics
    _____ Ch. 6: Science: Study Topics
    _____ Ch. 7: Don't Be Defeated by Multiple-Choice Questions
    _____ Ch. 8: Practice Questions
    _____ Ch. 9: Right Answers and Explanations for the Practice Questions
    _____ Ch. 10: Are You Ready? Last-Minute Tips

3. Are there parts of the study guide that you would recommend for removal in future editions of the guide?

    ☐ No   ☐ Yes

    If yes, which part(s)? _____

4. Are there any additions to the study guide that you would recommend?

    ☐ No   ☐ Yes

    If yes, please describe _____
    _____
    _____

5. Are there any other changes to the study guide that you would recommend?

    ☐ No   ☐ Yes

    If yes, please describe _____
    _____
    _____

6. Would you recommend this study guide to a friend who is preparing for the test?

    ☐ No   ☐ Yes

7. How many months before the test would you recommend that a person should start studying for the test?

    _____ month(s)

For more information about ETS Teaching and Learning, please visit us at *www.ets.org/praxis*.

THE **PRAXIS**
S E R I E S™

Thank you for taking the time to complete this feedback form. Please remove the page from the study guide, fold along the dotted lines, and seal with tape before mailing.
We look forward to hearing from you!

- -

Learning Tools
Mail Stop 20-D
PJ 510-54

ETS—The Praxis Series
P.O. Box 6058
Princeton, NJ 08541

- -

For more information about ETS Teaching and Learning, please visit us at *www.ets.org/praxis.*